SOUTHERN
CROSSINGS

GOURMET TRAVELLER

FIJI

INSPIRED ESCAPES + CULINARY JOURNEYS

FIJI

INSPIRED ESCAPES ✛ CULINARY JOURNEYS

CONTENTS

7   **INTRODUCTION**

8   **SOUTHERN CROSSINGS**
Curators of bespoke luxury culinary journeys.

12   **COMO LAUCALA ISLAND RESORT** Cakaudrove province.

26   **KOKOMO PRIVATE ISLAND** Kadavu archipelago.

40   **VOMO ISLAND** Mamanuca archipelago.

54   **SIX SENSES FIJI** Mamanuca archipelago.

68   **ROYAL DAVUI** Beqa lagoon.

82   **LIKULIKU LAGOON RESORT** Mamanuca archipelago.

96   **TOKORIKI ISLAND RESORT** Mamanuca archipelago.

110   **WAKAYA PRIVATE ISLAND RESORT & SPA**
Lomaiviti archipelago.

124   **NANUKU RESORT** Pacific Harbour.

138   **TURTLE ISLAND** Yasawa archipelago.

152   **JEAN-MICHEL COUSTEAU RESORT** Vanua Levu.

166   **VATUVARA PRIVATE ISLANDS** Northern Lau archipelago.

180   **YASAWA ISLAND RESORT & SPA** Yasawa archipelago.

194   **SOUTHERN CROSSINGS**
Owner and director, Sarah Farag.

195   **ACKNOWLEDGEMENTS**

196   **GLOSSARY**

198   **COOK'S NOTES**

199   **INDEX**

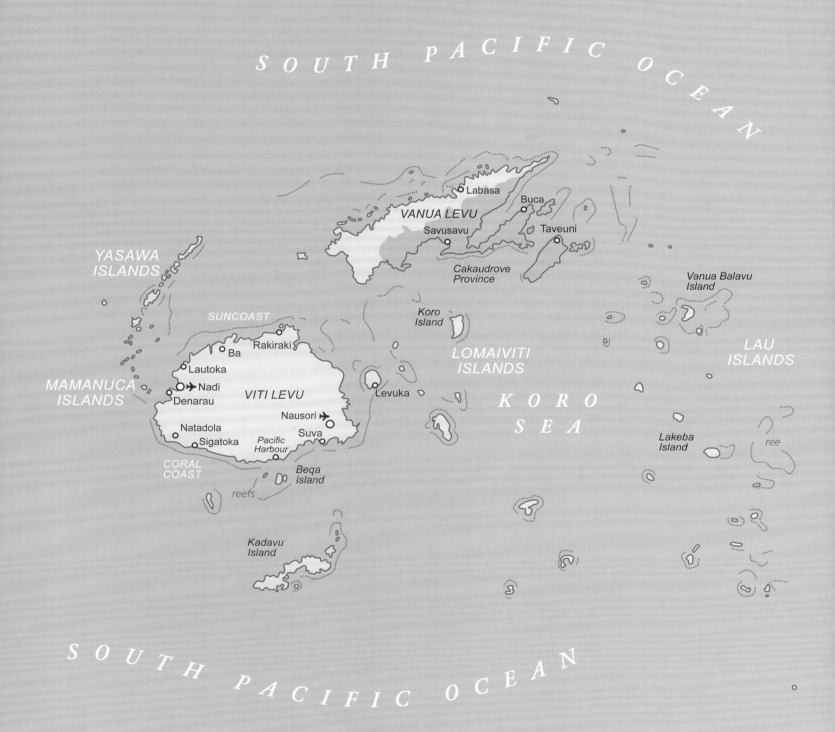

Rotuma Island

SOUTH PACIFIC OCEAN

VANUA LEVU

Labasa

Buca

Savusavu

Taveuni

Cakaudrove
Province

Vanua Balavu
Island

YASAWA
ISLANDS

Koro
Island

LAU
ISLANDS

SUNCOAST

Rakiraki

Ba

LOMAIVITI
ISLANDS

Lautoka

Nadi

VITI LEVU

KORO

Denarau

SEA

MAMANUCA
ISLANDS

Levuka

Nausori

Natadola

Suva

Lakeba
Island

Sigatoka

Pacific
Harbour

ree

CORAL
COAST

Beqa
Island

reefs

Kadavu
Island

SOUTH PACIFIC OCEAN

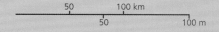

50   100 km

50   100 m

FIJI

Bula vinaka and welcome to the palm-fringed shores of Fiji
and its kaleidoscope of islands and islets in every shape and size;
where sand as soft as talcum powder meets the South Pacific surf
and time slows with every gentle breath. Inhale the fresh, sea air
and exhale away real life. Bask in the warmth of the sun, dancing on
your skin through dappled shade, and the charm of traditional
Fijian hospitality. No matter where you roam, you'll find yourself
warmly welcomed by local hosts who are proud to share their culture
with guests – through music, dance and, of course, food.

This travel-inspired *Gourmet Traveller* cookbook, created in partnership
with Southern Crossings, takes you into the kitchens of 13 of Fiji's
most luxurious resorts. While some of the featured properties feature
fine dining, others delve into regional traditions and family recipes. Each
captures the spirit of the archipelago, with a focus on tropical flavours,
sustainability and upholding traditions from fishing to farming.

We hope this book will remind you of happy holidays past and
serve as inspiration for future visits. Whether you seek a
multi-generational celebration, a romantic escape or a
restorative retreat, a befitting paradise awaits.

Southern Crossings pioneered the concept of bespoke luxury travel to New Zealand in 1986 with its vision to "enrich and inspire by creating extraordinary journeys". The dramatic and varied landscapes of this stunning part of the world provided a perfect canvas to create personally curated itineraries designed for the most discerning of travellers.

Four decades later, Southern Crossings still leads the way in tailoring holidays and unique travel experiences across New Zealand, Australia and the islands of Fiji. The essence of luxury travel has evolved over time and Southern Crossings has embraced this evolution. Today's sophisticated travellers want more than just luxury; they seek authentic, personalised experiences that offer the opportunity to connect with, and positively impact, the people and places they visit.

Local cuisine – and just as importantly, dining experiences – provide memorable connections to new destinations and cultures.

Fiji's culinary story is a celebration of culture and community, produce and provenance. The island-inspired cuisine draws on the nation's rich multicultural influences. Melanesian, Indian and European flavours and techniques meet on the menus of Fiji. The luxury resorts of Fiji elevate the region's culinary offering with well-travelled and highly-awarded chefs designing their menus around the day's catch brought in by local fishermen and seasonal produce grown in organic kitchen gardens.

From traditional Lovo feasts and shared bowls of Kava to secluded beach picnics and treetop dinners, it's with great care and pride that the team at Southern Crossings use their insights and connections to match travellers with experiences to suit their personal preferences.

With more than 300 Fijian islands, and dozens of honeymoon hideaways, ultraluxe private getaways and family-friendly resorts to choose from, there is a tailored Fijian luxury destination

for every occasion and every type of traveller. The team at Southern Crossings ensure travellers find their perfect pace and place.

Southern Crossings' long-standing reputation as a trusted local luxury travel expert has earned a loyal following and numerous prestigious industry affiliations. Owners and Directors Sarah Farag and Stuart Rigg are internationally recognised for their personal travel expertise with a range of awards for their contributions to the industry.

The application of in-depth local knowledge and meticulous dedication to planning ensures every Southern Crossings' itinerary is designed to align with the client's individual needs while indulging his or her passions. Starting with a blank canvas, each journey incorporates the knowledge, insights and connections of the company's Travel Design team to curate one-of-a-kind luxury travel experiences that exceed the highest of expectations.

For more than 38 years, Southern Crossings has been designing memory-making journeys throughout New Zealand, Australia and the islands of Fiji. The Travel Design team generously share their experience and insights to inspire and delight sophisticated travellers, who also enjoy the privileges that flow from the strength of Southern Crossings' well-established industry relationships.

Take for example Fijian-born caterers Komal (pictured) and Sonali Swamy of Koko and Chai. Working with Southern Crossings, Koko and Chai delivers private chef catering experiences and events across New Zealand and the Pacific in celebration of Fijian flavours and hospitality.

From the first joyful "Bula" to the moving "Isa Lei" farewell song, the warmth of the Fijian people guarantees every traveller's first visit to Fiji is never their last. Southern Crossings introduces travellers to a diversity of delicious luxury Fiji travel experiences, each presenting its own unique taste of this most inviting tropical island nation.
southern-crossings.com

COMO Laucala Island Resort

On an untamed private island in the glittering Coral Sea, a 25-villa, all-inclusive haven combines intuitive service with style and serenity. The result is an experience where every wish is the resort's command.

Golf on the 18-hole championship course today? Or perhaps horseback riding on the beach at low tide? A dive, tennis, jet skiing? And when would you like your 60-minute massage? In the hands of a less-exceptional resort these choices could be confounding. But at COMO Laucala Island Resort limitlessness reads as resplendence. It helps that the sheer number of options is made more approachable by a dedicated Tau (Fijian for friend) skilfully making arrangements. Are you relaxed yet? You will be.

Pronounced la-tha-la, this far-flung island is 12-square kilometres of rainforest, fern groves, a former coconut plantation and beaches, surrounded by a spectacular protected reef. Purveyors of holistic luxury, COMO took on the resort, a fifth of the island's footprint, in 2021. This was COMO's first foray into Fijian waters, bringing with them their holistic hotel magic to the nation's north-east corner.

COMO Laucala Island Resort is more remote than other Fijian resorts, but those that make the journey deep into the archipelago are rewarded with beaches and diving spots they can have all to themselves. Getting there requires a 55-minute flight in a resort-owned plane from Nadi International Airport, stopping by the resort's luxurious transfer lounge. Or if you have a private plane, and many of the guests do, you can skip Nadi altogether and fly directly into Laucala (it's reported 20 per cent of guests arrive in this way).

On arrival you can retreat to your quarters, which is not merely a room but rather a standalone home on a stretched-out estate. The smallest of the 24 residences measures in at a glorious 800-square metres, and the largest, a three-bedroom plantation residence, is 8000-square metres, including its own private beach. All residences include a private pool, and they are all dressed to thrill in seagrass and billowing linens.

Guests who can tear themselves away from the villa may self-drive or be chauffeured around the property in their own golf buggy. First stop? The COMO Shambhala wellness retreat for restorative treatments in the hilltops. Then the farm, which supplies the restaurants with wagyu beef, poultry, honey, herbs and fresh vegetables.

Dining in each of the four venues is as nourishing as it is delicious. Island-grown produce stars alongside fish from local boats in the light and bright dishes, with all dining and most drinks (other than top shelf) included in the nightly rate. It's all part of a stress-free experience that leaves guests to float through their stay.

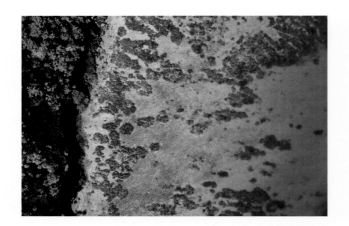

EXPLORE

Diving and snorkelling in the inner reef are possible at mid and high tides. Or head to the outer reef where remote dive sites are within a 45-minute boat journey. The resort offers PADI-certified dive instruction for all levels: even beginners can be certified within four days.

Thai green chicken curry with basil palm heart

SERVES 4 // PREP TIME 40 MINS // COOK 30 MINS

"The culinary journey of this dish brings the authenticity of Thai cuisine to Fiji," says Executive Chef Daniel Boller. "I feel blessed that I can pick fresh sustainable ingredients from my herb garden and use farmed chicken and home-grown vegetables from the island." This recipe makes double the green curry paste you will need for the dish; leftover curry paste stores well.

500 ml coconut cream
500 ml chicken stock
600 gm chicken thigh fillets, cut into thick strips
200 gm small eggplant, cut into small chunks
200 gm snake beans, cut into 1cm lengths
½ medium red capsicum (200gm), sliced
½ medium yellow capsicum (200gm), sliced
6 small makrut lime leaves
400 gm can hearts of palm, drained, cut into small cubes
10 gm (1 cup) Thai basil
1 tbsp fish sauce
Steamed jasmine rice, to serve

GREEN CURRY PASTE
3 tsp white peppercorns
1½ tsp coriander seeds
1 tsp cumin seeds
30 gm shrimp paste, roasted (see note)
3 red birdseye chillies, seeds removed, chopped
4 long green chillies, seeds removed, chopped
50 gm galangal, chopped
2 bunches coriander, roots, stalks and leaves
2 lemongrass stalks (white part only), chopped
8 makrut lime leaves, finely shredded
2 red shallots, chopped
60 gm garlic cloves, coarsely chopped

1 For green curry paste, place peppercorns, coriander and cumin seeds in a small frying pan over medium heat. Cook, shaking the pan frequently, until fragrant and toasted (3-5 minutes). Grind in a spice grinder or pound with a mortar and pestle until finely ground, then pass through a fine sieve and discard any large pieces. Place ground spices with remaining ingredients in a food processor and pulse for 1 minute or until well blended. Alternatively, pound ingredients, adding them one at a time, starting with the chillies, then the hardest ingredients, until a smooth paste is formed. Spoon paste into two jars and cover the surface directly with a piece of plastic wrap. Refrigerate until required or for up to 2 weeks or place in a freezeproof container and freeze for up to 1 month. Makes about 425gm.

2 To 'crack the coconut cream' remove thick cream from top of coconut cream and place in a large wok. Cook over high heat until it starts to separate (5 minutes) then add half the curry paste (200g) and cook until fragrant (2 minutes). Add chicken stock, remaining coconut cream, chicken, eggplant, snake beans, capsicum and lime leaves. Cook until the chicken and vegetables are tender (8 minutes).

3 Stir through hearts of palm and three-quarters of the basil, then season with the fish sauce. The curry should taste hot and salty with the richness of the coconut milk. Serve with remaining Thai basil and steamed rice.

NOTE To roast shrimp paste, wrap it in foil and roast at 200°C until fragrant (5-10 minutes).

DRINKS MATCH The trick with aromatic curry dishes that have spice is to find low-tannin and low-acid wines. Pinot grigio, soave and grüner veltliner fit this bill – as does a cheeky beer or cider!

Pork belly with cumquat jam and apple

SERVES 4 // PREP TIME 30 MINS (PLUS CURING) // COOK 11 HRS (PLUS PRESSING)

"There is nothing more rewarding than farming and harvesting fresh ingredients from your farm and designing menus from that," says Executive Chef Daniel Boller. "This recipe is the perfect pairing of sweet and tart cumquats and salty crisp-skinned pork belly: it will take you on a farm-to-plate journey." You will need to begin this recipe 2 days ahead.

200 gm rock salt
1 tsp ground white pepper
1 tbsp dried thyme
1 tbsp dried rosemary
1.2 kg pork belly, skin-on
1 litre vegetable oil (reserve 2 tbsp to finish)
250 ml extra-virgin olive oil
2 sprigs each fresh thyme and rosemary
1 fresh bay leaf
Micro greens (snow pea sprouts and nasturtium), to serve

CUMQUAT JAM
500 gm cumquats
450 gm caster sugar
200 ml orange juice

GARNISHES
1 small white onion (80gm)
2 tsp extra-virgin olive oil
1 Granny Smith apple, peeled

1 To cure pork belly, combine rock salt, white pepper and dried herbs in a bowl. Scatter half the salt mixture over the base of a small non-reactive container just large enough to hold the pork (the salt will not cover the base). Place pork skin-side down over salt mixture, then scatter with the remaining salt mixture. Cover and refrigerate to cure (overnight).

2 Remove pork from cure mixture and rinse. Pat dry with paper towel then set aside. Discard cure mixture.

3 Preheat oven to 80°C. Place pork in a roasting pan just large enough to hold the pork. Add oils, herb sprigs and bay leaf, then cover with foil. Transfer to the oven and cook until very tender (10 hours).

4 Carefully remove pork from cooking mixture and place on a tray lined with baking paper. Cover with another piece of baking paper and tray, and top with food cans or a heavy chopping board to weigh it down. Refrigerate to press and cool (overnight).

5 Meanwhile, for cumquat jam, slice cumquats and remove seeds, then place seeds in muslin cloth. Combine sugar, orange juice and 200ml water in a large saucepan over medium heat, stirring to dissolve sugar. Add cumquats and bag of seeds (these will add natural pectin). Cook until the mixture reaches 105°C on a sugar thermometer (about 45 minutes). Pour jam into sterilised jars (see Cook's Note, p 198). Cumquat jam will keep in sterilised jars for 3 months. Makes about 2½ cups.

6 For garnishes, cut onion into 5mm-thick slices, then separate slices into rings and toss with oil. Heat a greased char-grill pan over medium heat. Cook onion rings, turning until charred (1½-2 minutes). Using a melon baller, scoop balls from apple and place in acidulated water to prevent browning (see Cook's Notes, p 198).

7 To serve, cut pork into four, 5cm x 12cm lengths. Heat reserved vegetable oil in a large, non-stick ovenproof frying pan over medium heat. Cook pork, skin-side down, until skin crisps. Turn pork over and transfer to 180°C oven and cook until warmed through (5-6 minutes). Drain pork on paper towel.

8 To serve, divide pork among serving plates. On the opposite side of each plate, spoon around jam. Divide apple balls among plates and garnish with micro greens.

MAKE AHEAD Cumquat jam can be made up to 3 months ahead.

DRINKS MATCH For lovers of white wine, pick up an off-dry riesling, but for those wanting red, a chilled gamay or pinot noir will also work just as well to cut through the richness of the pork.

Green papaya pad Thai

SERVES 4 // PREP TIME 20 MINS (PLUS SOAKING) // COOK 10 MINS

"Green papaya pad Thai is one of our signature lunch dishes as it showcases a different style of eating papaya where the papaya replaces rice noodles," says Executive Chef Daniel Boller. "The best papaya I have ever tasted is here in Fiji."

125 gm tamarind pulp
600 gm green papaya
2 tbsp vegetable oil
100 gm firm tofu, finely diced
4 red shallots, thinly sliced
4 eggs
40 gm pickled turnip (preserved radish) (see note), cut into julienne
1 bunch garlic chives, cut into 2cm lengths
100 gm bean sprouts
1-2 tbsp lime juice, to taste
45 gm unsalted peanuts, roasted and crushed
Dried chilli flakes and lime halves, to serve

PAD THAI SAUCE
50 gm caster sugar
100 gm palm sugar, finely grated
300 gm tamarind purée (see recipe above)
60 ml fish sauce
60 gm tomato paste

1 For tamarind purée, combine tamarind pulp and 300ml hot water in a small bowl and leave to soak (15-20 minutes). Using your fingers, squeeze the tamarind to soften and break up the pulp until the mixture forms a thick purée. Push mixture through a fine sieve and set aside until required. Discard seeds.

2 For pad Thai sauce, place sugars in a medium heavy-based saucepan over low heat. Cook, stirring occasionally, until sugar dissolves. Add tamarind purée, fish sauce and tomato paste, and stir until combined. Bring to the boil for 2 minutes then set aside.

3 Peel the papaya, then using a vegetable shredding tool, peel into long noodle-like strands and set aside.

4 Heat a wok over high heat. Add 1 tbsp oil and stir-fry tofu until golden (2 minutes) then transfer to a paper-towel-lined plate. Add shallot and stir-fry until fragrant and starting to colour. Crack in the eggs and stir for a few seconds until they resemble an omelette (1 minute). Add pad Thai sauce and bring to the boil then cook until thickened slightly (1-2 minutes).

5 Add green papaya noodles, pickled turnip and three-quarters each of the fried tofu, chives and bean sprouts. Stir-fry until warmed through (2 minutes). Add lime juice to taste; toss to combine.

6 Spoon green papaya noodles among bowls. Scatter with remaining tofu, chives and bean sprouts. Sprinkle with peanuts and chilli flakes, and serve with lime halves.

NOTE Pickled turnip, also known as salted preserved/pickled turnip, is available from Asian food stores.

DRINKS MATCH A chilled and refreshing cider is an ideal pairing for this dish. The cider's apple and pear notes will cut though the richness of the pad Thai without being overwhelmed by the spice.

Kokomo Private Island

Escape to an unspoilt island in Fiji's south, surrounded by the Great Astrolabe Reef. Here, an ultra-luxe resort serves up pure bliss to couples and glam families intent on making the most of their downtime.

Touching down on Kokomo feels like being let in on a secret. An if-you-know-you-know oasis for those who wish to relax in uncompromised style, Kokomo is the Fijian dream, elevated. If you're there, you're in the community, most likely alongside rich listers and incognito luminaries as they enjoy time off with loved ones. Because at Kokomo, celebrities are just like you.

With only 26 Beachfront Villas and Grand Residences, the resort feels intimate and warm. This feeling is only enhanced by the Fijian welcome song performed by staff on arrival. Though, perhaps it's the long legacy of family holidays, which began when the late Lang Walker AO bought Yaukuve Levu island in 2012. Back then, it was an abandoned Aman project, but Walker raised it into a laidback-luxe getaway for discerning couples and groups, including his own multi-generational family.

Sustainability is key to the Walker family passion project. The farm, seawater desalination plant and recycling program keep the island as self-reliant as possible. Meanwhile, local fishing villages are supported by the island's dock-to-dish program, which teaches best-practice fishing protocol throughout the region. The resort's mangrove reforestation efforts also help to protect local low-lying villages from the threat of climate change. Guests can join the marine biology team in coral reforestation or even adopt a manta ray as part of the resort's conservation work. It's all about leaving Fiji a better place to visit.

Good work is rewarded with dreamy private digs. One-, two- and three-bedroom villas all hug the coastline, each enjoying a private patch of beachfront with either a sunrise or sunset view. All of these Fiji-chic villas include a pool, a deep soaking tub and generous touches such as laundry services and a complimentary mini-bar (often loaded with honeycomb from the island's own bees). Families will ease into holiday mode with the help of resort nannies, kids' club and teens' club – all included as part of the island's sophisticated-family MO. Venture further into the hills on a buggy to discover Kokomo's five ludicrously capacious Grand Residences, all serviced by a dedicated butler and nanny for extended families and groups.

But the true lure of Kokomo is the high-calibre dining. Think farm-fresh produce and just-caught local seafood, with live crustaceans cooked to order. At Kokocabana Pool Club woodfired pizzas and pastas reign, and at Beach Grill the fare is light, balanced and often kissed by fire. Then, at Walker D'Plank, Head Chef Caroline Oakley puts her Fijian heritage on show, plating up family-style dishes to bring people together.

EXPLORE

Spend the morning finding
equilibrium in the yoga pavillion
or just take in the splendour of the
island from the floating pontoon.
Each day on Kokomo Private Island
is enriched by local culture and song,
thanks to the warm and welcoming
Fijian staff members.

Chicken sang choi bau

SERVES 6 AS A STARTER // PREP TIME 15 MINS (PLUS SOAKING) // COOK 20 MINS

"This light starter is loved by all ages," says Executive Chef Andy Bryant. "The key elements are a sweet-and-sour flavour with crisp and crunchy goodness. Our Kokomo version is made with ingredients picked fresh from our organic farm garden."

1 small iceberg lettuce
50 gm uncooked glutinous rice
2 tbsp peanut oil
600 gm chicken thigh fillets, cut into
    1.5cm cubes
1 tbsp ginger cut into julienne
    (optional)
2 garlic cloves, finely chopped
2 tbsp fish sauce
1 tbsp light soy sauce (optional)
65 gm palm sugar, finely grated
2 tbsp lime juice
2 spring onions, thinly sliced
½ cup round-leaf mint
½ cup coriander leaves
    Chilli flakes and lime wedges,
    to serve

1 Turn the iceberg lettuce core-side up and run a knife around the core then discard core. This will make it easier to peel off the leaves. Remove leaves until you reach the smaller inner ones; you will need about 6 leaves. Trim leaves if necessary to make more bowl-like. Place iceberg lettuce leaves in a bowl of iced water to soak until crisp (1 hour), then drain well.

2 Meanwhile, for toasted rice powder, place rice in a small dry frying pan over medium heat. Stir continuously until rice begins to brown (5-7 minutes). Set aside to cool. Place rice in an electric spice or coffee grinder and grind to a gritty powder (like coffee grounds). Transfer to an airtight jar and store until required, or for up to 1 month.

3 Heat peanut oil in a hot wok over high heat. Add chicken, ginger, if using, and garlic, and stir-fry until fragrant (30 seconds to 1 minute). Add fish sauce, soy sauce, if using, and palm sugar. Stir-fry until the palm sugar dissolves and the liquid begins to thicken and caramelise the chicken, making it golden-brown and glossy (6-7 minutes).

4 Cool slightly, then toss through the lime juice, half of the spring onion and half of the herbs.

5 Divide chicken mixture among lettuce cups and top with remaining sliced spring onion and herbs. Sprinkle with toasted rice powder and chilli flakes. Serve with lime wedges.

MAKE AHEAD Toasted rice powder can be made up to 1 month ahead and stored in an airtight container.

DRINKS MATCH The stonefruit notes in a chenin blanc along with its freshness will work wonderfully with the flavours in this dish, refreshing the palate with every sip.

Chilli mud crab

SERVES 4 // PREP TIME 30 MINS // COOK 25 MINS

"This dish is a Kokomo classic, featuring freshly caught crab from the pristine waters that surround the island, which are blessed year-round with abundant seafood," says Head Chef Caroline Oakley. "Fiji is known for its fiery dishes, and this dish is both sweet and savoury at once. It's balanced with just the right amount of spice cooked to each guest's preference."

2   **live mud crabs (about 1kg each, see note)**
2   **tbsp fish sauce, plus 60ml extra**
2   **egg whites**
½   **tsp ground white pepper**
140   **gm potato starch**
  Vegetable oil, to deep-fry, plus 2 tbsp extra, to cook
6   **red shallots, thinly sliced**
3   **long red chillies, thinly sliced on the diagonal**
20   **gm (4cm piece) ginger, finely grated**
6   **garlic cloves, finely chopped**
85   **gm tamarind purée**
60   **ml lime juice**
100   **gm sriracha (Thai hot chilli sauce)**
120   **gm palm sugar, finely grated**
250   **gm tomato medley mix**
  Holy basil, coriander leaves and steamed rice, to serve

1 Kill crabs humanely (see note). Lift the abdominal flap underneath, then remove and discard. Holding the bottom end, pull away the top shell and reserve. Remove and discard gills and twist off claws. Using a cleaver, cut the body of each crab into quarters. Crack the claws with the back of the cleaver or a meat mallet, this will allow the flavours to permeate the crab meat and will make it easier to eat. Repeat with the second crab.

2 Whisk 2 tbsp fish sauce, egg whites and pepper in a large bowl to combine. Add crab pieces and toss to coat. Sift over potato starch to coat, then toss again.

3 Half fill a wok with vegetable oil and heat to 200°C, or until a cube of bread browns in 5 seconds. Deep-fry the crab claws and pieces, in batches, turning over once or until golden brown (3 minutes). Add the reserved top crab shells and fry until they turn red (10 seconds). Drain in a bowl lined with paper towel and keep warm.

4 Drain oil from wok and clean. Add 2 tbsp extra oil to clean wok and heat over medium heat. Stir-fry shallot, chilli, ginger and garlic until fragrant (30 seconds). Add tamarind purée, lime juice, sriracha, palm sugar and 60ml extra fish sauce, tasting and adjusting to balance the sweetness, saltiness and spice of the sauce.

5 Bring sauce to the boil. Add crab pieces and tomatoes, and toss continuously until well coated in the sauce (2-3 minutes).

6 To serve, divide chilli mud crab and sauce between two large bowls. Top each with a crab shell. Scatter with holy basil and coriander and serve with steamed rice.

NOTE RSPCA recommendations for killing crustaceans humanely is to first render the crab insensible by placing it in the freezer, then inserting a knife into its head to destroy its nerve centre.

DRINKS MATCH Chilli is always hard to pair wine to as it exacerbates tannin and acid in the mouth, so a change in thinking is required. A refreshing and bubbly long cocktail, such as a Tom Collins or mojito, or even a simple gin and tonic, will cool you down.

Barbecued lobster with 'nduja butter and toasted nori

SERVES 2 // PREP TIME 30 MINS // COOK 10 MINS (PLUS PREHEATING)

"Our Fijian lobsters are incredibly sweet, and we love to prepare them over the barbecue with very light Mediterranean flavours," says Head Chef Caroline Oakley. "Our recipe is a simple combination of 'nduja butter and nori; it's very easy to prepare, and delivers a delicious salty, umami flavour to bring out the taste of the lobster."

50 gm 'nduja (see note)
125 gm salted butter, at room temperature
½ tsp smoked paprika
Zest and juice of ½ lemon
6 nori seaweed sheets
2 live rock lobsters (about 900gm each)
Coastal sea herbs or succulents, to serve

1 For 'nduja butter, combine 'nduja and butter in a small bowl until well combined and smooth. Stir in smoked paprika and lemon zest until combined, then season to taste with sea salt. Refrigerate until required.

2 Heat a large non-stick frying pan over medium heat. Cook nori sheets, turning once until crisp (5 seconds each side). Immediately, break nori sheets into small pieces, then using a spice or coffee grinder, blend to a powder. Transfer to a sealed jar. Makes 2 tablespoons.

3 Kill lobsters humanely (see note). Remove heads by twisting and pulling the tail and head in opposite directions, discarding heads. Using a heavy knife, cut the tail in half, then remove digestive tract. Cover and refrigerate until required.

4 Heat 'nduja butter in a small saucepan over low heat until melted.

5 Heat a barbecue or char-grill pan to medium-high. Brush cut-side of lobsters with a little 'nduja butter and season with salt. Place lobsters, cut-side down, on the barbecue or grill until shells begin to change colour (3-4 minutes), then turn and brush with a little more 'nduja butter. Grill until flesh turns opaque (3-4 minutes).

6 Transfer lobster halves to a platter, spoon over a little more 'nduja butter and season with lemon juice. Garnish with a dusting of nori powder and coastal sea herbs or succulents. Serve with remaining butter passed separately.

NOTE 'Nduja (pronounced en-doo-yah) is a spicy spreadable salami from Calabria. Made with a mix of pork, herbs and spices including a generous hit of Calabrian chilli peppers, it packs a punch. It is available from delis and specialty food stores. Scoop 'nduja from the casing, then fold the casing to use as a cover, before wrapping in plastic wrap and placing in an airtight container and storing leftovers for up to 1 month. RSPCA recommendations for killing crustaceans humanely is to first render the crab insensible by placing it in the freezer, then inserting a knife into its head to destroy its nerve centre.

MAKE AHEAD Leftover nori powder can be combined with a few toasted sesame seeds and sea salt and used as a seasoning to sprinkle over seafood and salads.

DRINKS MATCH Seek out rich and opulent Champagnes to pair with the complexity of this dish, in particular blanc de blanc (chardonnay) and blanc de noir (pinot noir) styles.

Vomo Island

Spread over not one tropical private island but two, Vomo is a five-star haven where connection and disconnection are intrinsically linked. Check in for a world-class escape and check out feeling renewed.

At 87 hectares, Vomo is one of Fiji's larger private islands and among its most luxurious. The resort is in the Mamanuca archipelago, 15 minutes by helicopter from Nadi International Airport or a little longer by speedboat.

On Vomo, guests want for nothing. Couples and small families can settle into one of 34 outstanding villas, whilst larger groups can indulge in any of the six multi-room beachfront residences with private pools and butler services. Answering the question "What could be better than a private tropical island?" Vomo has two. It's second, smaller island Vomo Lailai (Little Vomo) is reserved for just one couple each day to be "marooned" with a gourmet picnic hamper and a two-way radio to use when they decide to be "rescued".

On the food front, Vomo is renowned for its cuisine and all meals at two restaurants are included. The approach is clean and green "plantation to plate" cuisine where daily changing menus are curated to suit the tropical environment perfectly. All part of the experience.

At the Vuda Reef Restaurant, the day starts as you peruse a chilled room displaying breakfast treats, whilst barista coffees and cooked selections are delivered with a smile. Dine at the seashore for lunch, wrapped in your sulu (sarong) under shady palms. In the evening the elegance is elevated with menus fusing the traditional with contemporary, all accompanied by serenading guitars.

On the western tip of the island with ocean views at every head-turning angle, the Rocks Bar & Restaurant is the place for poolside "rocktails" and canapés in an adults-only chill zone. The vibe here is relaxed, serving up surprising share-plates from South East Asia, India, the Mediterranean and Fiji, changing each night. Zealous waiters will want to help order for you but beware incredible dishes that seemingly never stop arriving.

Those with children make use of the Kids Village, which has its own chef. It's a favourite place for kids to gather for early dinner, sans parents. All families are gifted four hours of Baby Butler babysitting each day – so every night can be date night.

While heartfelt Fijian hospitality is prioritised here, so too is the fragile environment. The island includes its own water bottling plant and employs a unique E-water system for chemical free cleaning, while food waste is turned into garden fertiliser. Young guests can join the eco-spirit too, with the island's marine biologist showcasing eco practices that include coral planting and turtle nurturing in a bid to improve on perfection.

EXPLORE

Head out on a Vomo Lailai day picnic to the resort's little sister island for an adventure the resort describes as "Survivor luxury style". Picnickers will have an entire island to themselves, plus sun loungers, a gourmet picnic and a two-way radio to call when they want to be rescued.

Prawn ceviche (ura konda taki)

SERVES 4-6 // PREP TIME 30 MINS (PLUS MARINATING)

"Traditional ura konda taki sees savoury prawns bathed in citrus juice to 'cook' the prawns," says Executive Chef Ajay Dahiwale. "Combined with the sun-ripened pineapple, it captures the essence of the Pacific, showcasing the bounty of local produce."

500　gm medium sashimi-grade green prawns, peeled and deveined (see note)
250　ml lime juice
　　1　small red onion (100gm), finely chopped
　　1　small red chilli, finely chopped
450　gm yellow-fleshed pineapple, peeled and finely diced
200　gm cherry tomatoes, finely diced
　½　cup coriander leaves, chopped
　　　Olive oil, to serve
　　　Banana leaf cut into strips and micro coriander, to serve

1 Cut prawns into bite-sized pieces and place in a non-reactive bowl. Pour over the lime juice, ensuring prawns are fully submerged. Cover and refrigerate until the lime juice 'cooks' and denatures the proteins (60 minutes). The prawns will turn opaque and have a firmer texture.

2 Drain lime juice from prawns and discard juice.

3 Add red onion, chopped chilli, pineapple, tomato and coriander to prawns, and mix well to combine.

4 Season ceviche with sea salt and freshly ground black pepper to taste, then return ceviche, covered, to the fridge for flavours to meld (15 minutes).

5 To serve, place a banana leaf strip on each plate, then place a 9cm ring mould on top and fill with prawn mixture. Press down firmly to fill the ring, then carefully lift away the ring. Repeat on remaining plates, scatter with micro coriander and drizzle with oil.

NOTE It is important to source sashimi-grade prawns, as the acidic marinade will denature the proteins resulting in a similar texture as if heated, however since they aren't actually cooked freshness is paramount for safety.

DRINKS MATCH To mix up your pairings, seek out a sparkling riesling from Australia or Germany. Otherwise, classic matches such as sauvignon blanc and other aromatic white wines will work well.

Drunken prawns

SERVES 4 // PREP TIME 30 MINS (PLUS DISGORGING) // COOK 25 MINS

"Plump local prawns are enhanced by a fragrant broth of citrus-led herbs and the gentle heat of ginger in a light and refreshing broth," says Executive Chef Ajay Dahiwale. "Creamy just-cooked eggs and crisp cucumber add contrasting texture."

2 eggs, at room temperature
Lemon balm and edible flowers, to serve

DRUNKEN PRAWNS
250 ml Shaoxing wine
15 gm turmeric, thinly sliced
30 gm ginger (4cm piece), thinly sliced
6 makrut lime leaves, crushed
1 stalk lemongrass (white part only), sliced thinly
20 large green prawns (about 750gm), peeled and deveined

SMASHED CUCUMBERS
2 Lebanese cucumbers (150gm each)
Juice of 1 lemon
3 tsp olive oil
2 tsp soy sauce
1 tsp sesame oil

1 For drunken prawns, place Shaoxing wine, turmeric, ginger, lime leaves, lemongrass and 3.5 litres water in a saucepan over medium heat. Cook until flavours develop (15 minutes). Strain and return liquid to saucepan.

2 Meanwhile, for soft-boiled eggs, bring a small saucepan of water to the boil. Gently lower eggs into the water, return to the boil and simmer until soft-boiled (4½ minutes). Plunge eggs into a bowl of iced water until cool enough to handle, then carefully peel and set aside until required.

3 For smashed cucumbers, place a cucumber on a chopping board and smash it gently with the flat side of a cleaver or heavy knife a few times until it splinters and opens up with jagged edges. Repeat with second cucumber, then cut each cucumber into bite-sized pieces and place in a bowl. Sprinkle with ½ tsp salt and leave to disgorge (15-20 minutes), then drain and place the cucumber in a bowl.

4 Add prawns to the poaching liquid from step 1 and simmer gently until just cooked and changed in colour (4-5 minutes).

5 Using a slotted spoon, divide prawns among bowls then ladle over a little poaching liquid.

6 Add remaining smashed cucumber ingredients to cucumber in the bowl and toss gently to combine. Season to taste.

7 Serve prawns topped with half a soft-boiled egg. Garnish with lemon balm and edible flowers, with cucumber salad passed separately.

DRINKS MATCH As this is a refreshing, light dish, lightweight wines are the best match, such as pinot gris from the cool-climate Mornington Peninsula in Victoria.

Spiced rum tuna gravlax

SERVES 4 // PREP TIME 20 MINS (PLUS 2 DAYS CURING)

"Infused with local rum, while allowing the bright flavours of the tuna to shine, our Fijian version of gravlax is served topped with a jewelled medley of citrus. It's a taste of the tropics for a starter or shared plate experience," says Executive Chef Ajay Dahiwale.

4 **baby cucumbers, sliced lengthways on a mandoline**
Lemon zest and salmon caviar, to serve

GRAVLAX
500 **gm sashimi-grade tuna (see note)**
2 **tbsp sea salt flakes**
1 **tbsp unrefined sugar**
90 **ml Ratu spiced rum (see note)**
1 **tsp freshly ground black pepper**
1 **bunch dill, half finely chopped, remaining picked into sprigs, to serve**
Zest of 1 lemon

CITRUS SALAD
1 **orange**
1 **lemon**
1 **ruby grapefruit**
1 **tbsp extra-virgin olive oil**

1 For gravlax, rinse tuna and pat dry with paper towels. For cure, combine sea salt, sugar, spiced rum, black pepper, finely chopped dill and lemon zest in a bowl.

2 Place a large piece of plastic wrap on a work surface and sprinkle a little of the cure mixture. Lay the tuna on top, then evenly coat the entire surface of the tuna with the remaining cure mixture. Tightly wrap the tuna in plastic wrap, twisting the ends of the plastic to tighten and create a compact log shape. Place in a shallow container and refrigerate to cure (48 hours, turning the tuna every 12 hours).

3 On the day of serving, make citrus salad. Trim top and base of citrus slightly and then, with the fruit upright, cut the rind away with as much of the white pith as possible. As you cut, follow the curve of the fruit. Hold the fruit, one at a time, over a bowl and cut down each side of the segment, close to the white membrane. Squeeze grapefruit membrane to release 2 tbsp juice into a separate bowl. Repeat with lemon to yield 2 tsp juice, then finish with the orange membrane to release 1 tbsp juice. Whisk olive oil into juice mixture and season to taste. Cut citrus segments into bite-sized pieces and add to dressing. Set aside until required.

4 Unwrap the tuna and gently scrape off the cure mixture. Thinly slice tuna at an angle.

5 Arrange gravlax tuna on plates and top with cucumber ribbons, citrus salad and dressing. Serve with dill sprigs, lemon zest and salmon caviar.

NOTE It is important to source sashimi-grade tuna, as the acidic marinade will denature the proteins, however since they aren't actually cooked freshness is paramount for safety. Fiji Ratu spiced rum is aged in charred oak barrels, filtered through coconut-shell carbon. The rum is flavoured with vanilla, orange, cinnamon and star anise. You can substitute another spiced rum.

DRINKS MATCH With some complex flavours in this dish, it's best to allow the gravlax to shine by choosing some more neutral wines — think gruner veltliner or pinot blanc from the Adelaide Hills in South Australia.

MAMANUCA ARCHIPELAGO

Six Senses Fiji

International design values meet hyper-local sensibility on a sparkling private island. Enter a five-star boutique retreat that wants to help you live your best beach life.

There's a bar in the Six Senses Wellness Village in Fiji where scrubs and masks are mixed to your mood. You can also experience Alchemy Bar, the Six Senses signature move in Portugal's Douro Valley, and in the Swiss resort town of Gstaad where you can be slathered with bespoke potions as part of an après-ski treatment. On Malolo Island, 45 minutes from Nadi by boat or 10 minutes by helicopter, ingredients are plucked from the resort's own gardens. These include hibiscus, neem leaves, papaya and, if you feel the need to fend off jet lag, local medicinal herbs known as vevedu and vau. In the mix, it's a beautiful way to recalibrate.

Fans of Six Senses properties have come to expect this level of engagement. After all, the brand was built on the concept of connection, providing opportunities to detach from distraction, awaken the senses and be in the moment. When the group announced its first Fiji property would open in 2018, the same fans knew refined aesthetics and a jaw-dropping location would follow. And they did, in the form of a 48.5-hectare gem fringed by a 650-metre private beach and a turquoise lagoon, dripping with wow factor.

But luxury on Six Senses Fiji runs deep. The resort is powered exclusively by solar and it desalinates its own drinking water. Produce is grown on site, while the resort's forested areas are also a haven for 39 critically endangered crested iguanas. This dedication to conservation makes the island an eco-conscious playground for hiking, diving, water sports or just watching the tide go in and out, cocktail in hand.

Those who resist the snooze button in favour of self-improvement can start their day with Hatha yoga. Guests who choose to journey further into wellbeing can adopt a targeted wellness program, which kicks off with a high-tech screening. Others can get their glow back in the Wellness Village via a 24k gold leaf facial.

There are enough guests opting into the wellness protocols to ensure clean eating is a possibility at all five restaurants on site, although house-made indulgences are on offer too. Tovolea Restaurant is the flagship where you can try fresh and thrilling dishes with a Pacific twist, including kokoda, a coconut cream ceviche. At Rara the menu is international but still favours local ingredients.

This place-centric approach extends to the 24 villas and the smattering of three-to-five-bedroom residences, which all feature their own pools. Inside each guest space, reeded walls blend with high-tech speakers, and Sleep With Six Senses mattresses and bedding are optimised for deep slumber. In fact, the bed is so luxurious it makes yoga at sunrise seem unlikely.

EXPLORE

Head to Alchemy Bar in the Wellness Village to discover Fiji's traditional remedies. Concoctions can be tailored to your goal, be it sleep, stress reduction or energy, and applied during spa treatments. Meanwhile, children are engaged in craft and cooking through the Grow With Six Senses program. Surfing and watersports are on also on offer.

Cured scallops with fermented marinated kiwifruit

SERVES 4 // PREP TIME 25 MINS (PLUS FERMENTATION, REFRIGERATION)

"My recipes are inspired by all the islands I have worked on, from Far North Queensland to Fiji. While our dishes are non-traditional Fijian food we source a variety of local produce," says Executive Chef Winston Fong. "We follow Six Senses Fiji's food ethos of 'less is more', using pristine local, sustainable and natural ingredients." You will need to start the recipe 3 days ahead.

Pink rock salt and 2 tsp Sichuan
peppercorns, to serve
Micro herbs, to garnish

FERMENTED KIWIFRUIT
50 gm caster sugar, plus extra to whisk
    with kiwifuit and chardonnay vinegar
50 gm sea salt
3   green kiwifruit
1   tbsp chardonnay vinegar (see note)

CURED SCALLOPS
2½ tsp sea salt flakes
    Zest of 1 lemon
12 extra-large scallops, in the half shell,
    roe removed

MARINATED KIWIFRUIT
4   green kiwifruit,
    peeled and thinly sliced
2   tbsp freshly squeezed mandarin juice
2   tbsp yuzu juice (see note)

1 For fermented kiwifruit, combine 500ml water, sugar and salt in a small saucepan and stir until sugar and salt dissolve. Set aside to cool. Meanwhile, wash kiwifruit, rubbing away any fuzz. Trim ends from kiwifuit and discard. Place kiwi in a bowl, then gently crush with a fork. Transfer crushed kiwi to a sterilised jar (see Cook's Notes, page 198), then pour over brine to cover. Fill a small plastic bag with water and seal, place in the jar to keep kiwifruit submerged. Seal jar and set aside for 3 days to ferment. Strain, discarding brine. Add fermented kiwifruit to a bowl and whisk in chardonnay vinegar and extra sugar to taste. Set aside until required.

2 For cured scallops, begin the recipe 30-40 minutes before serving. Combine salt and lemon zest in a small bowl. Loosen scallops from shells and add to the bowl. Turn scallops to coat in cure, cover and refrigerate to cure (30-40 minutes, depending on scallop size). Meanwhile, wash and reserve scallop shells to serve. Rinse cure from scallops.

3 Meanwhile, for marinated kiwifruit, place kiwifruit slices in a shallow container, just large enough to hold them. Combine mandarin and yuzu juice in a jug, then pour mixture over kiwifruit. Refrigerate for flavours to develop (30 minutes).

4 To serve, place pink salt on each plate and arrange three cleaned scallop shells on top. Thinly slice scallops into discs. Remove kiwifruit from marinating liquid and arrange with scallop slices in each scallop shell. Drizzle with a little fermented kiwifruit and kiwi marinating liquid. Scatter with Sichuan pepper and garnish with micro herbs. Serve immediately.

NOTE You can swap the chardonnay vinegar for other aged white wine vinegars. Yuzu is a tangy citrus fruit with floral notes. The bottled juice is available from select supermarkets and Asian grocers; if unavailable, substitute with lime juice.

DRINKS MATCH The delicate balance between savoury and fruit-driven elements in a grüner veltliner will work well with the layers of complex flavours in this dish.

Eye fillet with mushroom, artichoke, blueberry and burnt butter emulsion

SERVES 4 // PREP TIME 45 MINS (PLUS MACERATING) // COOK 1 HR 20 MINS

"This is our go-to dish when it comes to creating comfort food woven with a bit of island flair," says Executive Chef Winston Fong. "It is full of umami flavours from the porcini, bresaola and browned butter, layered with the vegetal artichoke purée, cut with the sweetness of blueberries. It's a combination that our repeat visitors rave about."

4 eye-fillet steaks (250gm each), at room temperature
   Olive oil, to cook
   Truffle oil and chervil, to serve

MACERATED BLUEBERRIES
1 tsp sea salt flakes
1 tsp caster sugar
1 tsp red wine vinegar
125 gm blueberries, halved

PORCINI AND BRESAOLA POWDER
100 gm sliced bresaola (see note)
25 gm dried porcini

ARTICHOKE PURÉE
6 globe artichokes
1 lemon, halved
1 tbsp extra virgin olive oil
20 gm butter
2 tsp red wine vinegar
375 ml chicken stock

BROWN BUTTER EMULSION
150 gm unsalted butter, chopped
2 eggs, at room temperature
1 tsp Dijon mustard
2 tsp lemon juice

1 For macerated blueberries, stir salt, sugar and vinegar together in a bowl. Add one-third blueberries and crush with a fork. Cover and refrigerate for flavours to develop (2 hours). Place remaining blueberries in a small bowl. Strain blueberry juices over the blueberries in the bowl and discard solids.

2 For porcini and bresaola powder, preheat oven to 150°C. Place bresaola in a single layer on an oven tray lined with baking paper, then bake until dried (1 hour, turning halfway). Cool, then crumble into pieces. Blend porcini and bresaola to a powder using a spice or coffee grinder, then strain through a fine sieve. Discard any large pieces. Transfer powder to an airtight jar and store in the freezer until required or for up to 1 month. Makes 65gm.

3 Meanwhile, for artichoke purée, trim artichoke stalks to 2cm and snap off tough outer leaves until you reach the pale, tender inner leaves. Using a small, sharp knife, trim bases by cutting down the length of the stem to remove the outside of the stalk. Trim 2cm from the top of each artichoke and halve lengthways, then immediately rub cut surfaces with lemon. Using a teaspoon, scoop out hairy, fibrous choke and discard. Slice artichokes into wedges. Place one-third artichokes in bowl of water with lemon halves. Heat oil and butter in a large frying pan over high heat, cook remaining artichokes, turning occasionally until golden brown (4-5 minutes). Deglaze pan with vinegar and simmer until almost dry (1 minute). Add stock and simmer until reduced by two-thirds (4-5 minutes). Blend artichokes in a blender until smooth, then pass through a fine sieve into a small saucepan. Set aside until required. **4** For brown butter emulsion, place butter in a small saucepan and simmer over low heat until it changes to a nut brown colour; set aside. Allow the milk solids to settle then strain off the clear butter. Whisk eggs, then strain through a fine sieve into a small bowl. Place the bowl over a saucepan of gently simmering water (ensuring the base of the bowl doesn't touch the water) and whisk continuously until the egg begins to thicken (4 minutes). Immediately place the bowl over a second bowl of iced water and whisk to arrest cooking. Remove bowl from the iced water, whisk in mustard, then gradually whisk in browned butter, drop by drop at first, until starting to thicken, then in a slow steady stream until emulsified to a mayonnaise consistency. Add lemon juice and season to taste.

5 Pat steaks dry with paper towel, then rub well with sea salt flakes. Heat a heavy-based frying pan over high heat, then add 1 tbsp oil. Add the steaks and cook for 3 minutes each side for medium, depending on the thickness of the steaks. Transfer steaks to a tray, brush with truffle oil, then rest loosely covered and in a warm place for 5 minutes.

6 Meanwhile, drain and pat remaining artichoke dry. Heat 1 tbsp olive oil in a small frying pan over medium heat. Add artichoke and cook, turning occasionally until golden brown (4-5 minutes).

7 Spoon artichoke purée and brown butter emulsion onto plates and top with steaks and sautéed artichoke. Scatter with porcini and bresaola powder, and chervil. Spoon over blueberry mixture to serve.

NOTE Bresaola is air-dried beef fillet available from delicatessens.

DRINKS MATCH Time to bring out the cabernet family — cabernet merlot, cabernet franc. Wines with blue-fruit spectrum pair well with the flavours in the dish, and nice tannins cut through the beef.

Kingfish sashimi with almond cream, lemongrass and makrut-lime leaf oil

SERVES 4-6 // PREP TIME 40 MINS (PLUS INFUSING) // COOK 15 MINS (PLUS SOAKING)

"Everything about this dish follows the Six Senses food ethos," says Executive Chef Winston Fong. "It can be seen in the freshly caught kingfish, handled minimally, and the use of natural vibrant flavours such as island coconuts, to the lift from lemongrass and makrut lime, and the unexpected creaminess of the nut cream."

400 gm sashimi-grade Hiramasa kingfish
     Fresh coconut curls and micro lemon
     balm and red shiso, to serve

MAKRUT-LIME LEAF OIL
16 single makrut lime leaves
60 gm coconut oil

ALMOND CREAM
150 gm blanched almonds
1 garlic clove
2 tsp extra-virgin olive oil
3 tsp white wine vinegar

LEMONGRASS SYRUP
100 gm light palm sugar, finely grated
10 gm ginger (2cm piece), sliced
1 stalk lemongrass, white part only,
   bruised
1½ tbsp fish sauce
3 tsp mandarin juice
3 tsp lime juice

1 For makrut-lime leaf oil, blanch lime leaves in a saucepan of boiling water for 30 seconds until they turn bright green. Remove with a slotted spoon and plunge into a bowl of iced water. Drain, pat dry and finely chop. Blend chopped lime leaves in a spice grinder to a powder. Heat coconut oil in a microwave-safe bowl for 30-40 seconds until hot. Add lime leaf powder and stir to combine, then set aside for flavours to infuse (4 hours). If it sets, reheat for 10 seconds in the microwave, then strain through a fine sieve into a bowl.

2 Meanwhile, for almond cream, place almonds in a heatproof bowl, pour over 150ml boiling water, cover and set aside until cooled. Transfer almonds and soaking water to a high-speed blender with garlic, olive oil and vinegar, then blend to a smooth thick cream consistency (5-8 minutes). Season to taste then transfer to a piping bag with a plain nozzle. Makes 1½ cups.

3 For lemongrass syrup, place palm sugar, 100ml water, ginger and lemongrass in a saucepan over medium heat. Cook, stirring, until mixture boils and sugar dissolves (10 minutes). It should have a syrupy consistency. Set aside to cool, then strain into a jug and stir though fish sauce and citrus juices. Makes ¾ cup.

4 To serve, thinly slice kingfish sashimi into 5mm-thick slices. Arrange slices, slightly overlapping, in a single layer on plates. Drizzle with lemongrass syrup and top with piped rounds of almond cream. Add droplets of makrut-lime oil into the almond cream rounds. Garnish with fresh coconut curls and micro herbs.

MAKE AHEAD Makrut-lime leaf oil, almond cream and lemongrass syrup can be made a day ahead.

DRINKS MATCH No need to mess with a good thing when it comes to pairing with raw seafood dishes. Crisp aromatic whites such as a Clare Valley riesling, Hunter Valley semillon or Adelaide Hills sauvignon blanc are your go-to drops.

Royal Davui

If you're looking for a place to stow away to, Royal Davui Island Resort is it. Days on this adults-only island play out in a progressive game of pampering, adventure, relaxation and world-class dining.

Small but perfectly formed, there are just 16 thatched villas and bungalows on Royal Davui, a blissful boutique stay catering to no more than 32 guests at a time. Lapped by the stunning Beqa Lagoon, the petite island spans four lush hectares. To holiday here (with no public access) is to hand yourself over to a castaway experience made luxe. No crowds. No noise, other than nature's chime. Just beauty, privacy and feeling like you have the whole island to yourself.

Royal Davui Island Resort is an adults-only oasis accessed by helicopter from Nadi International Airport (35 minutes) or speedboat from Pacific Harbour (45 minutes). Once onshore, time slows and stress melts away as the body acclimatises to the rhythms of the all-inclusive experience.

The Pacific Rim ethos is deeply ingrained here. The owners, descendants of five generations of Fijians, built and launched the resort in 2005 and reside on-site. Working with the local chiefs, a one-kilometre marine sanctuary encircling the island was established, resulting in an abundance of marine life. Much of the team comprises locals residing in the staff village on the island, while others commute from nearby villages by boat daily from Beqa Island. It's these dedicated individuals who shape the island's serene ambiance, infusing it with the genuine warmth of Fijian hospitality honed to perfection. This extends into the culinary domain, where an entirely Fijian food and beverage team brings a wealth of family recipes and traditions to the dining experience.

Papaya, cumquat and pineapples are cultivated in the island's own soil, sourced alongside treasures from local fishermen and farmers. Collaborations with village suppliers underscore the resort's commitment to preserving traditional food production methods. This shines through on the Fijian fusion menu at Banyan Bar and Restaurant from the excellent à la carte breakfasts to multi-course lunches and dinners. Guests can dine free-range, enjoying the evolving menu in private dining spots including beach huts and hidden sand cays. Or dine in the villa, a secluded thatched-roofed haven with its own pool and private outdoor spaces.

Days unfold languidly from swims, walks and water sports to golf, cocktails and kava ceremonies. And while the views alone offer relaxation, guests would be well advised to drift over to the Davui Spa, where treatments are designed by Pure Fiji. Indulge in a Fijian Bobo massage or a body scrub using coconut milk and natural cane sugar followed by Pure Fiji Body Butter – surely the most sublime way to ease into the holiday zone.

EXPLORE

Dine on a daily-changing menu of modern Fijian cuisine in one of the resort's private dining spots. Settle into a romantic beach hut or delight in dinner in your own secluded thatched-roofed villa where you can conclude the meal with a private star-lit dip in the pool.

Steamed prawn and chicken dumplings with black vinegar sauce

SERVES 6 // PREP TIME 45 MINS // COOK 20 MINS

"A beloved favourite – succulent locally sourced prawns enveloped in a delicate dumpling, imparting natural sweetness," says Royal Davui Founder Christopher Southwick. **"Complemented with a touch of acidity from the black vinegar sauce, this dish is light, tangy, and ideal for a delightful lunch or dinner starter."**

500 **gm green prawns, peeled, cleaned, halved**
250 **gm chicken thigh fillets, chopped**
4 **spring onions, thinly sliced**
2 **tbsp finely grated ginger**
3 **tsp sesame oil**
3 **tsp light soy sauce**
¼ **tsp raw sugar**
1 **tsp cornflour**
270 **gm packet square wonton skins (Shanghai wrappers, see note)**
Rectangles of banana leaf (optional), to serve
Micro shiso (optional), and black and white sesame seeds, to serve

BLACK VINEGAR SAUCE
125 **ml Chinkiang (Chinese black vinegar)**
2 **tbsp vegetable oil**
¼ **cup coriander leaves, finely chopped**
1 **small red chilli, seeds removed, finely chopped**
1 **tbsp finely grated ginger**
1 **tsp light soy sauce**

1 Place prawn, chicken, spring onion, ginger, sesame oil, soy, sugar and cornflour in the bowl of a food processor. Pulse until mixture is finely chopped. Season with salt and ground white pepper.

2 Working with one wrapper at a time, place wrapper on a chopping board then place 1 tbsp of filling just off centre of wrapper. Brush edges with a little water, then fold over into a triangle, pressing out air and sealing edges together to form a dumpling. Place on a tray lined with baking paper, cover with a tea towel, and repeat with remaining filling and wrappers to make about 30 dumplings in total. Dumplings will keep refrigerated, wrapped in plastic wrap and covered with a tea towel, for 2 hours.

3 For the black vinegar sauce, whisk ingredients together in a small bowl until well combined. Makes 180ml.

4 Line a bamboo or stainless-steel steamer with baking paper, then pierce holes in the paper with a metal skewer. Place steamer basket over a large saucepan of boiling water. Add the dumplings and steam, covered, in batches until wrappers are slightly translucent and filling is cooked through (4-5 minutes).

5 To serve, place dumplings on a piece of banana leaf, if using, then top with micro shiso, if using. Serve dumplings with sesame seeds and black vinegar dipping sauce.

NOTE Wonton skins are available from select supermarkets and Asian grocers.

DRINKS MATCH A rosé brimming with red fruits will work wonderfully as a contrast to the black vinegar sauce. Refreshing acidity in the wine will pair well with the richness of the prawns dumplings.

Steamed snapper with ginger, soy and sesame

SERVES 2 // PREP TIME 15 MINS // COOK 20 MINS

"Sourced from the cool 400m ocean depths outside the Beqa Barrier Reef, our Pakapaka Snapper is steamed to perfection and infused with the classic trio of ginger, soy, and sesame," says Royal Davui Founder Christopher Southwick. "Fresh, tasty, and light — the epitome of a perfect tropical meal."

2	snapper fillets (about 180gm each), skin on
25	gm ginger, cut into julienne
2	spring onions, thinly sliced, plus extra to serve (see note)
1½	tbsp Shaoxing wine
1½	tbsp light soy sauce
1½	tbsp peanut or vegetable oil
1	bunch water spinach, thick stalk ends trimmed (see note), cut into 12cm lengths
1	garlic clove, finely chopped
2	tsp sesame oil
½	long red chilli, seeds removed, thinly sliced
	Coriander and steamed rice, to serve

1 Line a heatproof plate with baking paper, ensuring the plate fits snugly into a large steamer. Place fish, flesh-side up, on the plate and scatter over ginger and spring onion. Drizzle with Shaoxing and soy sauce, and cover and steam over a wok of boiling water until fish is cooked through (8-10 minutes).

2 Meanwhile, heat 1 tbsp peanut oil in a large frying pan or wok over high heat. Add water spinach and garlic, and stir-fry until wilted and bright green (2 minutes).

3 Heat sesame oil and remaining 2 tsp peanut oil in a small saucepan until smoking (1-2 minutes). Transfer fish, skin-side up, to serving plates, and drizzle over steaming juices. Pour over hot oil and scatter with extra spring onion, chilli and coriander. Serve with rice and water spinach.

NOTE Cut the spring onion tops into julienne and place in a bowl of iced water for 10 minutes to curl. Drain, pat dry on paper towel. Depending on the Asian grocer you source water spinach from it is also known as ong choy in Cantonese, kangung in Malaysia and Indonesia, kangkong in the Philippines, phak bung in Thailand and rau muong in Vietnam. Despite the name, this leafy green vegetable with edible hollow stems is, in fact, not a spinach but belongs to the convolvulaceae (morning glory) family. If unavailable use a bunch of gai lan instead.

DRINKS MATCH Delicate chardonnay such as a chablis will work wonderfully as it has less oak expression and more orchard fruits and hints of minerality.

Beef tartare with capers, mustard, cornichon and egg yolks

SERVES 4 // PREP TIME 30 MINS

"This is a French classic featuring local beef from Yagara, Fiji's oldest cattle region," says Royal Davui Founder Christopher Southwick. "The rich combination of flavours: capers, red onion, mustard and cornichon synchronise with the beef, creating a symphony of taste and texture. It's crowned with a luscious egg yolk, and just a hint of truffle oil to subtly elevate the rich flavour."

60	ml olive oil
2	tbsp Dijon mustard, plus extra to serve
1	tbsp red wine vinegar
50	gm capers, finely chopped
1	tsp Worcestershire sauce
1	tsp sambal oelek (see note)
450	gm beef tenderloin
2	tbsp flat-leaf parsley, finely chopped
50	gm golden shallot, finely chopped
4	refrigerated eggs
12	cornichons
	Truffle oil, to serve
4	slices toasted baguette

1 For dressing, combine olive oil, mustard, red wine vinegar, capers, Worcestershire sauce and sambal oelek in a large bowl. Season with sea salt and pepper and set aside.

2 Cut beef into 5mm pieces. Add beef to dressing with parsley and shallot, and stir to combine. Taste and adjust the seasoning if necessary. Cover the beef mixture directly with plastic wrap if not serving immediately to prevent oxidation and refrigerate.

3 To serve, place a 10cm ring mould on a serving plate and fill with a quarter of the beef mixture. Using the base of a clean egg, press into the beef mixture to make a well in the centre. Separate the egg and place the yolk in the well. Reserve egg whites for another use. Add a smear of extra Dijon mustard and cornichons and drizzle with truffle oil. Serve with toasted baguette.

NOTE Sambal oelek is a Malaysian and Indonesian chilli paste with visible seeds and a slightly chunky consistency. It is available from supermarkets and Asian grocers. Substitute another chilli paste or sauce.

DRINKS MATCH For a match made in culinary heaven, chilled reds are the ultimate go-to with beef tartare. Pop a bottle of gamay, pinot noir or nebbiolo in an ice bucket as you devour.

Likuliku Lagoon Resort

This secluded adults-only hideaway is the home of Fiji's first over-water bures. Head to Likuliku Lagoon Resort for a feelgood blend of romance and conservation, with magic moments on repeat.

Marooned on stilts in the Mamanuca Islands in a utopian overwater bure, a glass-panelled floor reveals the under-water action below. Watch this window long enough and you might spot Fiji's mythical "box of blessings", which, according to legend, was lost in these waters by seafaring warrior Chief Lutunasobasoba, bringing abundance to Likuliku and its neighbours to this day.

With a ladder into the lagoon, and nothing other than a winding boardwalk connecting the bures to shore, there might be no better way to wait out reality for a while.

Romance is the obvious goal at this ante-upping all-inclusive hideaway, and indeed there is a lot to love here. The resort was the first to introduce over-water accommodation to Fiji, while the on-land offering is modelled on a traditional village in the style the Fijian owners grew up with. Beyond the 10 exclusive stilted bungalows, there are also 35 spacious beachfront bures (18 with plunge pools), all featuring woven natural materials and South Pacific wood carvings to help guests attune to their borrowed surroundings. At the heart of it all is a Fijian canoe house. With soaring ceilings and a handwoven thatch, it's a throwback to the island's seafaring heritage.

This traditional canoe house is adjacent to Fijiana restaurant, Likuliku's central dining hub, where guests feast on clean and creative dishes, favouring fresh seafood and island-grown produce.

Rather than take ownership of this slice of mystical Malolo Island, the Fijian family that runs Likuliku's parent company Ahura Resorts became custodians of the land under a 99-year lease. Royalties and rent (based on a percentage of resort sales) are paid to the traditional landowners. And as caretakers, they treat the environment gently with a buffet of sustainability measures, including coral gardening, mangrove restoration and a breeding program for the resort's colony of crested iguanas, a critically endangered species.

Guests can take part in conservation projects or simply relax at the Tatadra Spa. Weekly cultural events like fire dancing and kava ceremonies bring the Fijian experience to the fore. Then it's a case of eating, drinking, basking by the water, and swimming with only the rising and setting sun keeping time. At holiday's end, the return trip to the real world is as simple as a 10-minute scenic helicopter flight or 25-kilometre boat transfer and short drive back to Nadi International Airport. But leaving this luxurious castaway island is never going to be easy.

EXPLORE

Head out early on an Island Hop tour to visit Monuriki island where the movie *Cast Away* was filmed. Likuliku guests arrive before all the other tours — so you have the place to yourselves (and your Wilson volleyball). Stunning scenery and snorkelling abound.

Seaweed tartlet with black truffle, mushrooms, warm potato and sweet peas

SERVES 6 // PREP TIME 30 MINS (PLUS INFUSING) // COOK 1 HR 50 MIN (PLUS INFUSING, DRYING)

"This elegant snack is layered with complementary flavours, encased in a crisp fillo shell flecked with seaweed," says Executive Chef Gregory Llewellyn. **"The potato truffle cream top is made with local potatoes and Parmigiano Reggiano."**

1 nori sheet
5 fillo pastry sheets
Cooking oil spray
40 gm cooked warm peas
Dried mushroom powder
Micro dill, to serve

KOMBU OIL
100 gm kombu (see note)
200 ml grapeseed oil

BARBECUE MUSHROOM MIX
200 gm oyster mushrooms
100 gm shiitake mushrooms, stalks discarded
60 ml garlic-infused extra-virgin olive oil
2 tbsp lemon juice
1 tbsp each finely chopped tarragon and chives

POTATO ESPUMA
360 gm potatoes, cut into 6cm pieces
360 gm milk
100 gm butter
100 gm finely grated parmesan
3 tsp truffle paste
¼ tsp xanthan gum

1 Place nori sheet in a hot frying pan and toast on each side (30-60 seconds). Cool, then chop into small pieces and blend in a spice or coffee grinder to a powder. Store in a sealed jar.

2 Spray a sheet of fillo pastry with oil spray, then cover with a second sheet. Spray with oil spray then cover with a third fillo sheet. Scatter with nori powder, then continue layering and spraying with remaining fillo to create a stack of five sheets. Cut pastry stack into six 14cm squares. Grease six 10.8cm fluted brioche tins. Press a fillo stack square into a tin, then place a second brioche tin on top, pushing down to ease pastry into corners. Repeat with remaining fillo squares, then, using scissors, trim excess pastry flush with the rim.

3 Preheat oven to 180°C. Place tart shells on an oven tray, then stack a second brioche tin inside pastry shell to prevent pasty rising. Bake until golden and crisp (20-25 minutes). Cool, then carefully remove pastry shells from tins.

4 For kombu oil, reduce oven temperature to 150°C. Place kombu on a small baking-paper-lined oven tray and roast until crisp (1 hour), then cool. Break into pieces, then process with oil in a blender until smooth. Leave to infuse for 1 hour, then strain through a fine sieve, pressing down on the sediment to release as much oil as possible. Kombu oil will keep refrigerated for up to 3 weeks. Makes ½ cup.

5 For mushroom mix, place mushrooms in a bowl, drizzle with oil and lemon juice, season with salt and toss well to combine. Set aside for flavours to infuse (30 minutes). Heat a barbecue or char-grill pan to high. Add mushrooms and barbecue, turning, until golden and cooked through (4-5 minutes). Set aside to cool, then finely chop and combine with tarragon, chives and 2 tbsp kombu oil.

6 For potato espuma, place potato in a saucepan of cold salted water and bring to the boil. Reduce heat to medium and cook until tender (10 minutes), drain well and set aside in a colander to dry for 10 minutes. Place a fine sieve over a bowl, then push potato through in batches. Place milk and butter in a medium saucepan over medium heat and stir until melted. Fold in sieved potato, parmesan and truffle paste, then season with salt. (The mixture will look wet and may look curdled at this stage). Place in a blender with xanthan gum and blend on low speed for 1 minute until combined (see note). Spoon into a piping bag fitted with a plain nozzle.

7 To serve, warm fillo tart shell and mushroom mixture separately. Place fillo shells on plates, fill with mushroom mixture, then top with warm peas. Spoon over warm potato espuma and dust with mushroom powder. Garnish with dill.

NOTE Kombu is dried kelp and prized for its high umami-inducing glutamates. It is available from Asian food stores. If you have a cream charger, you can express the potato espuma to aerate it even further.

MAKE AHEAD Kombu oil and fillo pastry shells can be made a day ahead.

DRINKS MATCH The umami notes in the tartlet are reminiscent of the earthy, whole bunch (stem and all) character often seen in cool-climate pinot noirs, such as the ones from the Yarra Valley or Tasmania.

Smoked Spanish mackerel with macadamia milk, salted radish and dill oil

SERVES 6 // PREP TIME 45 MINS (PLUS COOLING, BRINING, DRYING) // COOK 40 MINS (PLUS SMOKING)

"We use walu for this recipe. It has a dense fatty flesh that lends itself to being smoked in dried coconut husks then browned," says Executive Chef Gregory Llewellyn. **"The fish's texture and smoky notes, coupled with crisp radish pickles, pair well with the savoury macadamia milk and abundant herbs from the garden."** You will need to brine a day ahead.

600	gm walu (Spanish mackerel) fillet, skin removed
	Coconut husks (see note)
2	tsp vegetable oil
	Wilted water spinach or other greens, to serve

BRINE

160	gm fine sea salt
80	gm caster sugar

PICKLED RADISH

2	star anise
5	dried red chillies, crumbled
25	gm coriander seeds
125	gm white sugar
10	gm fine sea salt
50	gm ginger, sliced
500	ml white vinegar
150	gm radishes, sliced or quartered depending on size

MACADAMIA MILK

100	gm macadamias
¼	tsp xanthan gum
1	tbsp garlic-infused extra-virgin olive oil
1	tsp fine sea salt

DILL OIL

2	bunches dill
180	ml canola oil

1 For brine, place salt and sugar in a saucepan with 1.6 litres water, and bring to the boil, stirring to dissolve salt and sugar. Set aside in the fridge until brine has cooled to 5°C. Place fish in a shallow container and pour over brine, then refrigerate for no more than 1 hour. Remove fish from brine and discard brine. Place fish on a tray and place in the fridge, uncovered, overnight to dry out.

2 For pickled radish, place star anise, dried chillies and coriander seeds in a small dry frying pan over medium heat. Cook, stirring, until fragrant and toasted (3 minutes), then transfer to a saucepan with sugar, salt, ginger and vinegar. Stir over medium heat to dissolve sugar and salt, then boil for 2 minutes. Remove from heat and stand to allow flavours to infuse (30 minutes). Place radish in a bowl and strain liquid over radishes (discard solids). Refrigerate for at least 30 minutes or until required.

3 For macadamia milk, using a high-speed blender, blend 300ml water and macadamias for 1 minute, then strain through a fine strainer and discard solids. Return milk to blender with xanthan gum, garlic oil and salt. Blend on high speed for 1 minute, then set aside.

4 For dill oil, remove dill sprigs from large stems (you will need 2 cups) and wash thoroughly. Blanch dill in a saucepan of salted water for 1 minute, drain immediately and refresh in iced water. Drain well, then squeeze out excess water. Wrap dill in paper towel and squeeze dry again. Blend dill with canola oil and a pinch of salt until smooth and vibrant green then strain through a fine sieve. Refrigerate until required.

5 To smoke brined fish (see note), place a small oiled metal rack in a Dutch oven and place fish on top. Place the end of the smoking gun's hose in the Dutch oven and add a small amount of coconut husks into the burn chamber. Light the husks until you see smoke exiting the hose. Cover with a lid and stand 2-3 minutes. Repeat process five more times, emptying the chamber of husks and refilling.

6 Cut brined and smoked fish into 12 portions. Heat oil in a large frying pan over high heat. Add fish and cook, turning, until golden (2 minutes each side). Drain on paper towel.

7 To serve, place a little water spinach in each bowl and top with 2 portions fish, spoon macadamia milk around and arrange a few pieces of drained radish. Drop a little dill oil into macadamia milk.

NOTE Likuliku use dried coconut husks and a smoker. Here we have adapted the recipe to use a smoking gun which is an easy way to cold smoke a variety of foods. They are available online from specialty kitchen stores. If you don't have a smoking gun, line a wok with foil, combine 30g tea leaves and 2 tbsp brown sugar in the base and place an oiled rack on top. Heat until smoking (1-2 minutes). Working quickly, turn off the heat, place fish on rack then invert a second wok over the top and leave for 30 minutes.

DRINKS MATCH The addition of macadamia milk in this dish seeks out the buttery creamy notes of a Margaret River chardonnay.

Milk chocolate miso semifreddo with coffee crémeux

SERVES 12 // PREP TIME 45 MINS (PLUS REFRIGERATION) // COOK 55 MINS (PLUS INFUSING, FREEZING)

"This dessert started off simply as an ice-cream on a stick before evolving into a sophisticated plated dessert, with a milk chocolate shell providing crunch. The interior hides a milk chocolate semifreddo, a combination of blonde miso paste and Italian meringue," says Executive Chef Gregory Llewellyn. "The combination is savory, with a touch of bitterness from the coffee, balanced with a little flaked sea salt produced locally in Sigatoka – it is very fun to eat."

200 gm couverture milk chocolate, melted
Micro mint leaves, to serve

ITALIAN MERINGUE
100 gm caster sugar
75 gm egg whites (about 2)

MISO AND MILK CHOCOLATE SEMIFREDDO
140 gm milk chocolate (48% cocoa), chopped
40 gm white (shiro) miso paste
200 gm pouring cream

CHOCOLATE ALMOND CRUMB
75 gm ground almonds
60 gm plain flour
75 gm caster sugar
¼ tsp fine salt
75 gm unsalted butter, chopped
120 gm dark chocolate (70% cocoa), melted plus 30gm extra, melted

COFFEE CRÉMEUX
600 ml thickened cream
90 gm coffee beans
120 gm egg yolks (about 8)
90 gm caster sugar
40 gm cornflour

1 Place a spoonful of melted couverture milk chocolate into each hole of a 12 x 100ml silicone cylinder bar mould tray. Rotate tray to coat sides, then tip out excess chocolate. Refrigerate until set (30 minutes).

2 Meanwhile, for Italian meringue, place sugar and 60ml water in a small saucepan and stir over low heat (without boiling) until sugar dissolves. Simmer without stirring until syrup reaches 118°C on a sugar thermometer. Meanwhile, place egg whites in the bowl of a stand mixer fitted with a whisk attachment. Whisk over medium speed until soft peaks form. With the mixer running, carefully and slowly drizzle in hot sugar syrup. Increase speed to high and whisk until stiff and glossy. Set aside.

3 For semifreddo, melt chocolate in a bowl set over a saucepan of simmering water, then stir in miso until combined. Remove bowl from the pan, then gently fold in Italian meringue in two batches until just combined. In the clean bowl of an electric mixer, whisk cream to soft peaks, then carefully fold into the combined mixture in two batches. Spoon mixture into a piping bag and pipe into chocolate-lined bar moulds, then freeze until set (4 hours) or until required.

4 For chocolate almond crumb, preheat oven to 150°C. Place ground almonds, flour, sugar and salt in a bowl, then using fingertips, rub in butter and melted chocolate until small clumps form. Spread mixture over a baking-paper-lined oven tray and bake, running a fork through mixture every 5 minutes for 25 minutes or until lightly golden, to form a crumb. Taking care, transfer crumb to a bowl, then while hot, add extra melted chocolate and mix thoroughly. Spoon onto a clean baking-paper-lined tray and continue to mix as it cools to ensure a uniform crumb. Transfer to an airtight container and refrigerate until required.

5 For coffee crémeux, place cream and coffee beans in a saucepan and bring to just below boiling point, remove from heat and stand to infuse (30 minutes), then strain and discard beans. Whisk egg yolks and sugar in a bowl until smooth, then whisk in cornflour until well combined. Gradually pour infused cream mixture over egg yolk mixture, whisking to combine. Return mixture to pan and bring to a high heat, whisking continuously until mixture comes to the boil and thickens (5 minutes). Pour into a container and refrigerate until set (4 hours or overnight).

6 To serve, carefully unmould semifreddo onto chilled plate and sprinkle with sea salt. Place a spoonful of chocolate almond crumb to the side as a base. Using a hot dry spoon, quenelle coffee crémeux and place on crumb, then scatter with a little more crumb mixture. Garnish with micro mint.

MAKE AHEAD Semifreddo, chocolate almond crumb and coffee crémeux can be made up to 2 days ahead.

DRINKS MATCH This decadent dessert calls for an espresso martini or a cacao-infused Old Fashioned.

Tokoriki Island Resort

Intimacy and relaxed luxury set the tone on this boutique adults-only island encircled by a crystal-clear lagoon. Because at Tokoriki Island Resort, long-term romance is all but guaranteed.

If the hibiscus petals on the bed don't communicate it, the floating breakfast will: honeymoons and Tokoriki are meant to be. But there are also 25 coconut trees on this jewel box of an island that prove the attraction persists long after the first flicker. Each of these trees was planted by a couple on their 10th visit to the property. In fact, one couple has clocked in 58 visits and counting. For these frequent floppers, Tokoriki is still the one.

Privately owned by an Australian family for the past 29 years, Tokoriki Island Resort has made "relaxed luxury" its thing. Fifteen minutes from Nadi by helicopter or seaplane, or an hour by catamaran or speedboat, the adults-only bijou property accommodates a maximum of 72 guests at any one time. For those who can snare a spot, the resort brings warm Fijian hospitality and attention to detail to the beach.

A luxe take on Fijian style weaves through the freestanding absolute beachfront bures (some with pools) and larger beachfront pool villas. These are enveloped in lush tropical gardens to provide a private environment in which to capture the sunset from the double daybed or stargaze from the tropical outdoor shower after a late dip.

Dining is also an elevated take on Fijian culture, as Pacific and Asian cuisines influence the daily changing menus to feature passionfruit ceviche and cassava island fries.

Dine on fresh heart of palm, jicama, bora beans and rosella leaves, knowing you are providing income to farmers in Ba, Nadi and Sigatoka. Likewise, just-caught octopus and trevally offer succulence and support for fishermen from the Mamanuca and Yasawa Islands. In this spirit, the resort has worked with The Ministry of Agriculture to supply vegetable seeds to Tokoriki's local team to plant in their own homes at Yanuya village, ensuring the area's food future.

On the island, these efforts continue with Tokoriki's head gardener growing an array of tropical fruit, herbs and climbing spinach around the resort and in his nursery.

All this delicious dining sustains an active day of diving. The resort's award-winning PADI 5 Star Dive Centre is a lure for discerning adventure seekers in its own right, but it also plays into the island's sustainability story, taking part in giant clam regeneration and coral reef monitoring.

Alternatively, expel some energy playing tennis, on a guided nature walk, or with a visit to the nearby Yanuya Island village. Days can be spent on a four-hour secluded island picnic, relaxing poolside or unwinding with a sensational spa treatment. All good reason to keep coming back for more.

EXPLORE

Dining at Tokoriki can be as boundless as you like. Indulge in a floating breakfast, a private Champagne dinner on the jetty under the stars, or enjoy a couples' massage followed by dinner complete with serenaders.

Grilled lobster with Fijian asparagus and light coconut curry sauce

SERVES 4 // PREP TIME 40 MINS // COOK 25 MINS

"Set in an ideal location for seafood and with an abundance of natural resources, the flavours of the local ingredients really shine through here," says Chef Neori Mokotanavanua. "The delicate flavour of the local lobster and the crisp native asparagus marry perfectly with a creamy coconut curry sauce."

2 **lobster tails (about 200gm each), split lengthways, digestive tract removed**
100 **gm butter, melted**
1 **bunch asparagus (170gm), trimmed, blanched and refreshed (see note)**
Shaved toasted coconut and micro coriander, to serve

COCONUT CURRY SAUCE
2 **garlic cloves, coarsely chopped**
5 **cm piece ginger, coarsely chopped**
1 **lemongrass stalk (white part only), finely chopped**
10 **gm piece turmeric, finely chopped**
2 **tbsp coconut oil**
1 **medium onion (170gm), finely chopped**
2 **tsp yellow mustard seeds**
3 **tsp cumin seeds**
2 **tsp Kashmiri chilli powder**
1 **strip fresh curry leaves (22 leaves)**
1 **tsp curry powder**
1 **tsp tomato paste**
400 **gm can coconut milk**
1 **cinnamon quill**
¼ **tsp amchur powder (see note)**
1-2 **tbsp lemon juice, to taste**

CORAL TUILE
2 **tbsp vegetable oil, plus extra to cook**
1 **tbsp plain flour**
Few drops red food colouring

1 For coconut curry sauce, using a mortar and pestle (or spice grinder), pound garlic, ginger, lemongrass and turmeric to a paste. Heat oil in a large saucepan over low-medium heat until starting to shimmer. Add garlic paste mixture and onion, and cook, stirring occasionally, until onion is soft (5-7 minutes). Add mustard, cumin seeds and chilli powder, and stir until spices start to catch (1-2 minutes). Add curry leaves and powder and stir for a few minutes to combine. Add tomato paste and cook for 30 seconds until combined. Add coconut milk and cinnamon, and cook until flavours develop (5 minutes). Add amchur powder, then season with lemon juice, sugar and salt to balance flavours. Strain through a fine sieve then set aside and keep warm.
2 For coral tuile, place vegetable oil and 80ml water in a small bowl, then whisk in flour to form a thin batter. Add a few drops of food colouring to tint the batter. Heat a little extra oil in a frying pan over medium heat and add 1 tbsp batter. Cook until a lacy set pancake forms (1 minute). Using a spatula, carefully transfer to a baking-paper-lined oven tray to cool. Repeat with more oil and batter to make 6 tuiles in total.
3 For lobster, preheat oven to 180°C. Brush cut-side of lobster with butter. Preheat a char-grill pan or barbecue to medium-high heat. Add lobster tails in the shell, cut-side up, and cook until almost cooked through (3 minutes). Transfer to an oven tray and cook in the oven until just cooked through (5 minutes).
4 To serve, spoon warm curry sauce into wide bowls. Top each bowl with half a lobster tail, then place asparagus to the side. Serve lobster with toasted coconut, micro coriander and a coral tuile.

NOTE At Tokoriki they use duruka, a type of Fijian asparagus which has been substituted here with regular asparagus. Amchur powder is made from dried green mango and is used as a souring agent in curries. It is available from Asian food stores and spice stores.

DRINKS MATCH The creaminess of the lobster along with the creamy coconut curry can only call for one thing – a creamy, buttery chardonnay.

Ceviche of Spanish mackerel and passionfruit

SERVES 4-6 // PREP TIME 30 MINS (PLUS FREEZING, CURING)

"Set in one of the most beautiful resorts in the South Pacific, what more could you ask for than refreshing Spanish mackerel with the tang of passionfruit to complement this island-style dish," says Chef Thomas Lyons. "It is perfect accompanied with a chilled glass of wine while watching a magical Tokoriki sunset."

600   gm sashimi-grade Spanish mackerel (see note)
10   passionfruit (80gm each)
125   ml lime juice
    Zest of 1 lime
2   tbsp orange juice
1   tbsp honey
1   tbsp mirin
½   tsp sea salt flakes, crumbled
3   hot or mild green or red chilies, thinly sliced (Fresno, Jalapeño, Thai red chilies or Habanero)
1   small red shallot (50gm)
6   radishes
125   gm baby cucumbers, sliced
½   cup coriander leaves, chopped
60   ml coconut milk
    Chervil or micro coriander, to serve
    Chips of your choice: cassava, tortilla, taro or sweet potato, to serve

1 Place mackerel in the freezer for 30 minutes to firm (this will make it easier to slice).
2 Meanwhile, place pulp from 8 passionfruit into a small food processor and pulse to release the juice from the seeds. Strain through a fine sieve into a small bowl and discard seeds. You will need 125ml passionfruit juice. Remove pulp from remaining 2 passionfruit and set aside to serve.
3 Add lime juice, lime zest, orange juice, honey, mirin and salt to passionfruit juice, then whisk together to combine. Cut fish into thin slices and place in an airtight container, pour over passionfruit mixture, ensuring the fish is well submerged, then seal the container. Refrigerate for 30 minutes, stirring every 10 minutes to make sure all sides of the fish are cured by the liquid. The fish is cured once it is opaque. The longer the fish marinates the more the texture will change, becoming firmer.
4 Meanwhile, thinly slice chillies into rounds (retain the seeds for more heat, remove for less). Thinly slice the shallot and radishes into rounds, then place in a bowl of iced water with a small pinch of salt to crisp (for at least 20 minutes).
5 When the fish is ready, drain marinade over a bowl, then transfer fish to a large bowl. Drain red shallot and radish from iced water and pat dry on paper towel. Add to the fish, with the chillies, cucumber and coriander. Whisk coconut milk into reserved marinade and pour over ceviche, then stir to combine. Season with a little salt and pepper.
6 Divide mackerel ceviche among plates, then spoon a little reserved passionfruit pulp over the top and scatter with chervil or micro coriander. Serve chilled with chips.

NOTE It is important to source sashimi-grade fish as the acidic marinade will denature the proteins resulting in a similar texture to as if heated, however since they aren't actually cooked freshness is paramount. You can also use kingfish, snapper or other sashimi-quality fish.

DRINKS MATCH This dish's fresh and fruity flavours with a touch of tang means that sauvignon blanc will be your best bet.

Tarte au citron

SERVES 8 // PREP TIME 1 HR (PLUS RESTING, FREEZING) // COOK 1 HR 10 MINS (PLUS COOLING)

"The crisp pastry, zesty bitter-sweet filling and the caramel flavour of the meringue make for an unforgettable dessert. The candied watermelon rind adds such an interesting texture and dimension to this dessert," says Pastry Chef Orisi Kuribola.

Crumbled biscuits, thick cream and
micro lemon balm, to serve

SWEET DOUGH
150 gm unsalted butter
65 gm icing sugar, sifted
1 egg, at room temperature
300 gm plain flour
1 egg white

FILLING
4 eggs, plus 1 yolk
220 gm caster sugar
180 ml lemon juice
Finely grated zest of 1 lemon
250 ml pouring cream

CANDIED WATERMELON RIND
125 ml chardonnay vinegar
220 gm caster sugar
10 gm brown mustard seeds
5 cloves
1 cinnamon quill
1 tsp fennel seeds
200 gm watermelon rind (see note),
thinly sliced

MERINGUE
3 egg whites
200 gm caster sugar

1 For sweet dough, using an electric mixer fitted with the paddle attachment, beat butter, sugar and a pinch of fine salt until pale and creamy. Add egg and beat until just incorporated, then stir in flour. Turn out onto a work surface and lightly knead to bring together. Shape into a log and flatten into a rectangle, then enclose in plastic wrap. Refrigerate to rest (1 hour).

2 Meanwhile, for filling, whisk ingredients except cream in a bowl until well combined, then whisk in cream. Cover and refrigerate until required.

3 For candied watermelon rind, place ingredients and 60ml water in a small saucepan. Stir over medium heat until mixture boils and sugar dissolves. Reduce heat to low-medium and simmer until a light golden thickened syrup forms (20 minutes). Pour onto a baking-paper-lined oven tray, then using a fork, separate pieces and leave to cool.

4 Remove pastry from fridge and set aside for 20 minutes. On a lightly floured piece of baking paper, roll out pastry into a 3mm-thick, 20cm x 40cm rectangle. Use pastry to line a greased 10.5cm x 34.5cm rectangular loose-based tart tin, trimming excess pastry. Enclose excess pastry in plastic wrap and refrigerate. Lightly prick base of tart shell with a fork and freeze for 30 minutes.

5 Preheat oven to 180°C. Place tart shell on an oven tray. Line pastry with a large piece of foil and fill with pastry weights or rice. Blind-bake tart shell until edges are golden and pastry is set (30 minutes). Reduce oven to 170°C. Remove foil and weights, then bake until base is light golden and crisp (8-10 minutes). Repair any cracks or holes with excess pastry. Brush lightly with egg white and bake for a further 5 minutes. Cool.

6 Reduce oven to 150°C. Skim any foam from the top of the filling, then strain filling through a fine sieve into a jug. Carefully pour half the filling into tart shell. Place in the oven, then fill to the rim with the remaining filling. Bake until set around the edges with a slight wobble in the centre (20-25 minutes). Cool tart in tin for 2 hours, then remove from tin and cool completely (if you leave the tart in the tin for too long the pastry will sweat and lose the crispness).

7 Just before serving, make meringue. Place egg whites and sugar in the bowl of an electric mixer, then place the bowl over a saucepan of simmering water. Whisk with a hand-held whisk until sugar dissolves. Transfer bowl to an electric mixer and whisk on high speed until stiff and glossy (8 minutes).

8 To serve, spoon ¼ cup meringue into centre of eight plates, then spread into a strip. Spoon remaining meringue into a piping bag fitted with a plain nozzle, then pipe six rounds of meringue, slightly apart, three on each side of strip. Using a kitchen blowtorch, carefully caramelise meringue rounds and strip. Cut the tart into slices and position on meringue strip and top with a little candied watermelon rind. Place a few crumbled biscuits at one end of the plate and top with a quenelle of cream. Serve immediately garnished with lemon balm.

NOTE For watermelon rind ensure that none of the green skin or flesh remain.

DRINKS MATCH A late-harvest riesling, with classic citrus flavours and a softened acidity, would be a wonderful pairing with this tarte, a refreshing end to a meal.

Wakaya Private Island Resort & Spa

Legend and luxury cohabitate harmoniously. Touch down on the exclusive private island resort that made a pact to protect Fiji's natural resources and the richness of its culture.

There's a high point on Wakaya Island where majesty washes over. Awe-thirsty guests can hike here to take in the sunrise with a large dose of glomesh waters as the jungle stirs below. Legend has it, under threat of capture by invaders from a neighbouring village, the Wakayan Chief leaped to his death here to keep his island free. In his honour, the cliff now bears the name Chieftain's Leap to commemorate his sacrifice.

As the island stands today, the home of Wakaya Island Resort and Spa, the Chief of Wakaya would have a lot to be proud of. While the island was abandoned for a century, after an attempt at sugar farming didn't take off, villagers were enticed back in the 1960s, and hundreds of Fijians returned to build infrastructure for the boutique resort, including a church and school. They have since been joined by many more who have taken on meaningful work at the resort. This is in consultation with Fijian elders, who maintain indigenous traditions on the island, ranging from the artisanal to musical and medicinal.

Eyes are on the future too, as scientists and professors get to work on the property's environmental protection response across land and water.

With just 10 freestanding bures, the all-inclusive resort stays small to minimise its footprint on the 900-hectare island. The only way onto the island is via the resort's plane. Upon landing in Nadi, the team will escort you through immigration to a private Cessna Caravan to await your transfer in style. That is, unless you've docked in your super yacht and nabbed the single spot the resort allows for boats to drop anchor. This strictly limited approach means super yacht guests also have the run of the place.

Villas are as spacious as they are romantic, with soaking tubs, cathedral ceilings and Italian linens painting a picture of island decadence. And while the entry-level bures are luxurious in themselves, the top-level two- and three-bedroom villas blow expectations out of the water. Think private treatment rooms, infinity pools, personal chefs and on-call drivers ready to tend to the rich, famous and royal jetsetters who frequent these high-end digs.

Dining on the island is sustainable and sublime, with 70 per cent of ingredients grown on the island's organic farm or caught in its waters. Local chefs dip into their heritage to present riffs on traditions, such as lovo, the underground cooking technique passed down through generations, or kokoda, a local coconut milk ceviche. Paired with top-shelf wines, the meals are a delight. And fortunately so, as all the diving, fishing, hiking and golfing on offer makes for hungry work.

EXPLORE

Wakaya is just a short boat ride from some of the world's best coral reef spots. A true all-inclusive experience, one tank dive is included each day in the rate. Back on the surface, Fijian culture is central to life in the resort.

Kokoda ceviche

SERVES 6 // PREP TIME 35 MINS (PLUS MARINATING) // COOK 15 MINS

It is important to connect the ocean and the land where we are inspired by our own plentiful and pristine seafood and sun-ripened resources — it is truly a Fijian way of life, and a belief shared by our sous chefs Siteri, Emiou and Belo.

1	kg fresh white fish fillets (see note)
310	ml lemon juice
1	small red onion (100gm), finely chopped
¼	cup coriander, chopped
½	Bongo or red Habanero chilli, seeds removed, finely chopped
1	small Lebanese cucumber, finely chopped
1	small red tomato, seeds removed, finely chopped
375	ml coconut milk, chilled
100	gm yellow cherry tomatoes, quartered
3	fresh coconuts, water drained, halved Micro herbs, toasted coconut flakes, to serve

CASSAVA CHIPS

500	gm sweet cassava roots Vegetable oil, to deep-fry

1 Cut fish into 5mm-pieces and place in a glass bowl. Pour over 250ml lemon juice, then cover and refrigerate for the lemon to 'cook' the proteins in the fish (about 1 hour); the fish will become more firm and opaque.

2 Place red onion in a small glass bowl and pour over remaining 60ml lemon juice. Cover and refrigerate until fish is ready, then strain and discard the onion, reserving the infused juice.

3 For cassava chips, peel cassava then cut in half lengthways. Using a mandolin, cut cassava pieces, one at a time, into paper-thin slices. Place in a bowl of iced water for 20 minutes, then pat dry on paper towels. Preheat an air fryer to 180°C. Toss cassava slices in a bowl with a little oil to coat. Air fry, in batches, until crisp and golden, turning halfway through cooking time (6-8 minutes). Season with salt.

4 Strain the fish and discard the lemon juice. Place fish in a clean bowl with coriander, chilli, cucumber and chopped tomato, and stir gently to combine. Add onion-infused lemon juice and coconut milk. Season with salt and freshly ground black pepper.

5 To serve, divide kokoda among coconut halves, then top with cherry tomato, micro herbs and toasted coconut flakes. Serve immediately with cassava crackers.

NOTE Use Spanish mackerel, snapper, kingfish or other firm white sashimi-grade fish fillets. Kokoda (pronounced Ko-kon-da) should always be served chilled.

DRINKS MATCH A fruit-driven sparkling works wonderfully with this dish. Look towards prosecco and non-vintage Australian bubbles with plenty of fruity top notes.

Grilled fish Wakaya with spinach salad, thyme sauce and red wine sauce

SERVES 4 // PREP TIME 20 MINS (PLUS REFRESHING, INFUSING) // COOK 30 MINS (PLUS STANDING)

"With our fabulous underwater world and its produce on our shores, fish naturally takes pride of place on our menu, complemented by a rich array of produce grown in the nutrient-rich volcanic soil of our organic farm," says Head Waiter Henry.

120 gm baby spinach
    Juice of ½ lemon
  4 Spanish mackerel or other firm white
    fish fillets (250gm), skin on (see note)
    Wakaya or other sea salt
    (see note)
  2 thyme sprigs, plus extra to garnish
    Extra-virgin olive oil, to cook
 50 gm heirloom cherry tomatoes

    RED WINE SAUCE
100 gm cold butter, chopped
150 ml dry red wine
150 ml red wine vinegar
  1 tbsp black peppercorns, coarsely
    crushed
  1 tbsp finely chopped shallot
  3 tarragon sprigs
  1 thyme sprig

    THYME SAUCE
250 ml pouring cream
  2 thyme sprigs
 20 gm finely grated parmesan
 50 gm chilled butter, diced

1 For spinach salad, immerse spinach in a bowl of ice-cold water and stand until crisp (20 minutes). Transfer to paper towel or salad spinner to dry. Place dried spinach in a bowl, season with salt and pepper and lemon juice, then toss well to combine.
2 For red wine sauce, cook butter in a small saucepan over high heat until nut-brown (3-4 minutes) and set aside to cool. Meanwhile, place wine, vinegar, peppercorns, shallot, tarragon and thyme in a saucepan and bring to boil. Reduce heat to medium and simmer until liquid is reduced to 2 tablespoons. Remove pan from heat, stand for 10 minutes, then strain into a small clean pan. Discard solids. Reheat, then reduce heat to low, then gradually whisk in the cooled browned butter until combined. Season to taste. Set aside until required.
3 For thyme sauce, combine cream and thyme in a small saucepan and simmer gently over low heat until cream is reduced by half and thickened (8-10 minutes). Remove from heat, stir in parmesan until melted, then whisk in butter to thicken. Season to taste. Set aside until required.
4 Preheat a greased grill flat plate or frying pan to high. Season fish with Wakaya salt, freshly ground black pepper and thyme. Cook fish until just cooked through (2-3 minutes each side depending on the thickness of the fish).
5 Divide spinach salad among serving plates and top with fish. Garnish with thyme and spoon a little of each sauce on the side. Serve with heirloom cherry tomatoes.

NOTE Wakaya sea salt, sourced from green reefs of the Koro Sea, is dried on pristine beaches under the sun. Substitute with other unrefined sea salt. Spanish mackerel known by its Fijian name, walu, is revered in island cooking. If unavailable, substitute with barramundi, snapper or another firm white-fleshed fish.

DRINKS MATCH The smoky note of the grilled fish calls for a sauvignon blanc-based pairing either from New Zealand or a beautiful French expression from Sancerre.

Cassava cake

SERVES 16 // PREP TIME 30 MINS // COOK 1 HR 10 MINS (PLUS REFRIGERATION)

Fijian baking is inspired by seasonal vegetables and fruit to create a truly unique way of changing local produce into international cuisine. It's a challenge Kelera, Wakaya Island Resort's favourite Pastry Chef, takes up anytime.

CASSAVA CAKE

395	gm can sweetened condensed milk
400	gm can coconut milk
400	gm can coconut cream
385	gm can evaporated milk
1	kg sweet cassava roots, peeled, finely grated (see note)
150	gm caster sugar
3	eggs
3	egg whites
100	gm freshly grated coconut, plus extra to serve
	Rectangles of banana leaf (optional), to serve

TOPPING

80	ml reserved sweetened condensed milk (from above)
80	ml reserved coconut cream (from above)
80	ml reserved coconut milk (from above)
80	ml reserved evaporated milk (from above)
2	tbsp caster sugar
3	eggs

1 Preheat oven to 160°C. Grease a 23cm square cake tin, then line base and sides with baking paper.

2 Reserve 80ml each: sweetened condensed milk, coconut milk, coconut cream and evaporated milk for the topping.

3 For cassava cake, place remaining sweetened condensed milk, coconut milk, coconut cream and evaporated milk with remaining ingredients in a large bowl and stir well to combine.

4 Pour mixture into prepared tin and bake until just set (about 45 minutes).

5 Place reserved topping ingredients in a bowl with sugar, then whisk until sugar has dissolved. Whisk in eggs until combined without aerating. Pour topping over cake and bake until top is set (25 minutes). Cool cake slightly then refrigerate until chilled.

6 To serve, cut cake into 16 squares and place on a piece of banana leaf, if using, and top with extra grated fresh coconut.

NOTE If fresh cassava is unavailable, buy frozen cassava chunks. Thaw cassava then finely grate and squeeze out the excess liquid. Then substitute desiccated coconut for freshly grated coconut – the drier coconut will compensate for the wet frozen cassava.

DRINKS MATCH Time to double down on your coconut pairing with a modern version of a piña colada, which uses coconut water instead of cream to bring lightness to the drink while maintaining its tropical vibes.

Nanuku Resort

Intoxicating and luxurious all at once, Fijian ritual meets elevated cuisine in this dreamy escape. Located just beyond Fiji's mainland of Viti Levu, connected by a natural isthmus, it feels more remote than it actually is.

A grass-skirted warrior blows a conch shell like a trumpet. Another beats a wooden drum, known in these parts as a lali, to signal your arrival. Your itokani (buddy) is dressed in full Fijian dress as a village chief and he places a flower behind your ear. You are offered a fresh-picked young coconut to revive you from your journey, which was not as long as expected. And so begins your stay at Nanuku Resort, a two-and-a-half-hour drive from Nadi International Airport (unless, of course, you made use of the resort's private airstrip).

Caught between Pacific Harbour and jungle on Viti Levu's southern coast, 200 hectares of tropical lushness is fringed by a three-kilometre crescent of beachfront. The sandy beach is dotted with 13 villas, while 24 suites and residences are perched higher up to take in the endless views. Nanuku could get by on geography alone. Instead, it goes further to give guests the ultimate barefoot-luxury experience.

All accommodation here plays on traditional Fijian architecture, dialled up with outdoor showers, private pools and evening turndown services across the board. Families, groups and those who simply want to up the ante can book one of Nanuku's seven residences, including the six-bedroom Hilltop Residence. With its wraparound entertainer's deck, bar, kitchen and three plunge pools (which are just some of its bar-raising features), this is the property's largest and most exclusive digs.

With an all-Fijian cast of staff members, local culture is at the resort's core. It's the kind of place where customs feel baked in, not staged or sanitised for Western palates. Become enraptured as guests share in Fijian food safaris, fire walking and kava ceremonies.

With the local Batiwai tribe being known for fishing, Nanuku is mindful to protect these waters. On-site the sustainability manager and marine scientist leads The Batiwai Project, a program aimed at improving the local marine ecosystem, minimising the environmental footprint, and enhancing the wellbeing of Nanuku employees and the local community. Interventions include coral planting, reef conservation, mangrove tree planting and shore protection.

On the wellness front, spend a day at Nanuku's Lomana Spa and Wellness Centre, or take part in a boxing lesson or bootcamp. Parents can relax too as their children play in the Lailai Kids Adventure Club or build sandcastles with their nanny (children under 8 years old are designated their own).

At night, Nanuku's world-class stargazing is a highlight. View the sky via a NASA telescope and learn how Fijians have navigated the waters using the night skies and moon for thousands of years – just another immersion into this profound culture.

EXPLORE

Slip away to a neighbouring exclusive-use private island to enjoy a romantic chef-prepared Champagne picnic or an under-the-stars overnight camping experience. Access world-class surf breaks, snorkel the calm clear waters of Beqa Lagoon or visit a local market to collect the ingredients for a private lovo feast experience.

Goldband snapper, kai mussels and calamari with lolo sauce and crustacean oil

SERVES 4 // PREP TIME 40 MINS // COOK 2½ HRS

The delicate sweetness of snapper, mussels and calamari are perfectly balanced with a luxurious coconut sauce, while the crustacean oil adds to the essence of this dish, a magnificent celebration of seafood.

4   snapper fillets (about 160gm each), skin on
500 gm calamari
500 gm black mussels (kai), scrubbed, debearded
    Tarragon and chervil, to garnish

SHELLFISH BROTH
2½ tbsp vegetable oil, plus extra to cook
1   kg crustacean shells (lobster, crab or prawn shells or a mix), broken into pieces with any juices reserved
20 gm butter
1   each onion, celery stalk and carrot, finely chopped
1   small leek, finely sliced
½   fennel bulb, finely sliced
6   garlic cloves, bruised
2   tbsp tomato paste
200 ml brandy, dry sherry, or white wine
2   bay leaves
1   tsp coriander seeds, lightly crushed
4   thyme sprigs

CRUSTACEAN OIL
250 ml canola oil
½   each small onion, carrot, celery stalk, finely chopped
2   thyme sprigs
2   tsp tomato paste
125 gm prawn shells and heads

LOLO SAUCE (COCONUT SAUCE)
2   tbsp vegetable oil
1   white onion, thinly sliced
6   cloves garlic, finely chopped
2   lemongrass stalks (white part only), bruised with the side of a cleaver
3   cm (15gm) piece ginger, thinly sliced
½   bunch coriander stems, chopped
2   medium tomatoes, chopped
100 gm fish trimmings
800 ml coconut cream
    Lime juice, to taste

1 For shellfish broth, preheat oven to 180°C. Lightly oil a roasting pan with 2 tsp oil, add crustacean shells and spread out over pan. Roast until well coloured (30-35 minutes). Meanwhile, heat butter and remaining oil in a large saucepan or stock pot over medium heat. Add onion, celery, carrot, leek, fennel and garlic, and cook, stirring frequently, until vegetables soften (5-7 minutes). Add tomato paste and stir until darkened (30 seconds-1 minute). Add brandy, bay leaves, coriander seeds and thyme, then simmer until liquid is almost evaporated (3 minutes). Add roasted crustacean shells and 3 litres water. Simmer, covered, over medium heat for flavours to develop (1½ hours). Strain broth through a fine sieve into a clean saucepan. Makes 2 litres.

2 To reduce shellfish broth, bring to the boil, reduce heat to medium and simmer, uncovered until reduced by half (1 litre) (1½ hours). Reserve 375ml of the reduced broth for cooking squid and 60ml for steaming mussels.

3 Meanwhile, for crustacean oil, heat 2 tbsp oil in a small saucepan over medium heat. Add vegetables and thyme, and stir until softened slightly (4-5 minutes). Add tomato paste and stir until darkened (1 minute). Add prawn shells and heads, breaking up with the back of a spoon until coloured (3-4 minutes). Add remaining oil and heat gently for flavours to develop (50 minutes). Strain shellfish oil through a fine sieve over a bowl and set aside until required. Discard solids. Makes ¾ cup.

4 Trim snapper fillets, reserving trimmings. Remove innards from calamari by pulling tentacles from the body. Cut across head underneath eyes to separate tentacles in one piece (discard innards and eyes). Push tentacles outwards, squeeze beak out and discard beak. Slice off wings from body with a sharp knife. Remove skin by running your finger underneath the skin, separating it from the flesh, then peeling off in one piece. Discard skin. Remove backbone from tube, scrape and discard insides. Cut into thin rings, reserving the wings and tentacles with snapper trimmings for lolo sauce.

5 For lolo sauce, heat oil in a medium saucepan over medium heat. Add onion, garlic, lemongrass, ginger and coriander stem. Cook until fragrant and slightly caramelised (5-8 minutes). Add tomato and seafood trimmings, and cook, stirring, until well combined (1-2 minutes). Add coconut cream, bring to a simmer and cook until flavours develop (25 minutes). Strain through a fine sieve into a clean saucepan. Season to taste with sea salt and lime juice. Set aside until required. Makes 2 cups.

6 Place 375ml reserved shellfish broth in a small saucepan and bring to a simmer. Reduce heat to low, add calamari and cook until calamari is just tender (1-2 minutes). Set aside.

7 Place 60ml reserved shellfish broth in a medium saucepan and bring to the boil over medium heat. Add mussels, cover with a tight-fitting lid and increase heat to high. Cook, shaking pan continuously, until mussels have opened (3-4 minutes).

8 Add remaining shellfish broth to lolo sauce and reheat. Meanwhile, heat 1 tbsp vegetable oil in a frying pan and add snapper. Cook, skin-side down, until golden, then turn and cook other side (1½-2 minutes each side). Transfer to a tray and keep warm.

9 Divide snapper among serving bowls and top with calamari and herbs. Pour lolo sauce mixture and divide mussels around the fish. Add drops of shellfish oil into the lolo sauce to serve.

DRINKS MATCH Wines with saline minerality pair well with all the creatures of the sea: think Italian vermentino and Hunter Valley semillon.

Fijian fish curry

SERVES 4 // PREP TIME 25 MINS (PLUS SOAKING) // COOK 35 MINS

Rich in flavour and tradition, Fijian fish curry blends aromatic spices with seafood flavours to create a warming dish. Served with a coconut sambal featuring snapper, this curry is full of flavour and a wonderful reflection of culture and community.

800 **gm snapper fillets, cut into 3cm pieces**
Fried curry leaves, mixed chopped chillies, steamed basmati rice and tamarind chutney, to serve

CURRY BASE
150 **gm coconut milk powder**
40 **gm ghee**
5 **small red shallots, thinly sliced**
4 **garlic cloves, thinly sliced**
1 **sprig curry leaves**
2 **small green chillies, chopped**
1 **tsp fenugreek seeds, toasted, soaked in water for 5 mins (see note)**
1 **cinnamon quill, crumbled**
1 **tsp fennel seeds**
5 **cardamom pods, bruised**
2 **tbsp curry powder**
2 **tsp ground turmeric**
2 **tsp ground coriander**
2 **tsp ground cumin**
1 **tsp chilli powder**
500 **gm white fish frames, chopped, rinsed**

COCONUT SAMBAL
1 **small coconut, grated or 80gm desiccated coconut**
1 **tbsp Maldive fish (see note)**
1 **tbsp freshly grated turmeric**
3 **tsp chilli powder**
1 **small red onion, very finely chopped**
½ **tsp black peppercorns, crushed**
Juice of 2 limes

1 For curry base, whisk coconut milk powder with 750ml warm water, then set aside. Heat ghee in a large heavy-based saucepan until just starting to smoke. Add shallot, garlic, curry leaves and chilli, and cook until shallot is translucent (8-10 minutes). Add drained soaked fenugreek seeds and dry spices, and cook, stirring until fragrant (2-3 minutes). Add fish frame and cook, stirring, until opaque (3-5 minutes). Deglaze pan with 500ml water and simmer until nearly evaporated.
2 Add reconstituted coconut milk to the curry base and bring to the boil. Reduce heat slightly and simmer until well-flavoured (5-7 minutes). Remove from heat and stand for 10 minutes, then strain into a wide clean saucepan, discarding solids. Set aside until ready to serve.
3 For coconut sambal, place grated coconut, Maldive fish, turmeric, chilli powder, onion and black peppercorn in a mortar. Pound with a pestle until well mixed. Add lime juice gradually, stirring to combine, then season with salt. Set aside until ready to serve.
4 To serve, bring curry base to a gentle simmer over medium heat. Add snapper pieces, cover with a lid and simmer gently until just cooked (5-6 minutes).
5 Top fish curry with fried curry leaves and mixed chilli, and serve with steamed basmati rice, tamarind chutney and coconut sambal.

NOTE To toast fenugreek seeds, place in a small dry frying pan; stir over medium heat until fragrant (3-5 minutes). Maldive fish, or dried tuna, is available from Asian grocers.

DRINKS MATCH A light and aromatic pinot gris (or grigio) so as not to overpower the curry. The low acid in this wine will not clash with any heat from the dish.

Halwa crème brûlée with cardamom ice-cream

SERVES 6 // PREP TIME 45 MINS (PLUS INFUSING) // COOK 1 HR 10 MINS (PLUS REFRIGERATION, FREEZING)

Fijian food is multicultural, as showcased in this iteration of crème brûlée. It's an elegant dessert, infused with the sweetness of carrot and warmth of spice, plus the key flavours of the Indian dessert, halwa, rounded out with a silky cardamom ice-cream.

CARDAMOM ICE-CREAM

500	ml pouring cream
20	gm cardamom pods, bruised
4	egg yolks
85	gm caster sugar

HALWA CRÈME BRÛLÉE

560	ml pouring cream
240	gm cream cheese
1	small carrot (50gm), coarsely grated
3	cm piece ginger (15gm), peeled and thinly sliced
2	cinnamon quills
	Freshly grated nutmeg
5	egg yolks
90	gm caster sugar, plus extra sugar to brûlée
1	tsp vanilla extract
¼	tsp sea salt
25	ml dark rum

COCONUT TUILE

50	gm caster sugar
30	gm unsalted butter, at room temperature, plus extra to grease
1	egg white
35	gm plain flour
30	gm shredded coconut
	Grated lime zest, to serve

1 For cardamom ice-cream, bring cream and cardamom pods to just below boiling point in a saucepan over medium heat. Remove from heat and set aside to infuse (1 hour). Whisk egg yolks and sugar in a bowl until thick and pale. Pour in cream mixture and whisk to combine. Return mixture to pan and stir over low-medium heat until mixture thickens enough to coat the back of a spoon (5-6 minutes). Strain mixture through a fine sieve into a bowl and refrigerate until chilled. Churn in an ice-cream machine following manufacturer's instructions, then transfer to an airtight container and freeze until required. Makes 500ml.

2 For halwa crème brûlée, combine cream, cream cheese, carrot, ginger, cinnamon and nutmeg in a medium saucepan over low heat and slowly bring to a simmer. Reduce heat to low and simmer gently for flavours to infuse (10 minutes), then pass through a fine sieve and discard solids. Cool slightly. Combine egg yolks, sugar, vanilla and salt in a bowl and whisk until smooth. Gradually whisk in the cream mixture and rum to combine (avoid over-whisking). Pass through a fine sieve into a jug.

3 Preheat oven to 120°C. Place 6 x 200ml ovenproof dishes or ramekins in a roasting pan lined with a tea towel. Half-fill the dishes with the cream mixture and place the pan on an oven shelf. Finish filling the dishes to a few millimetres from the tops, then pour boiling water into the pan to come halfway up the sides of the dishes. Bake until set with a slight wobble in the centre (30-35 minutes). Remove brûlées from the pan and refrigerate for a few hours until chilled.

4 Meanwhile, for coconut tuile, draw a 5cm round on a sheet of firm plastic, then cut the shape out with a paring knife. Cut excess plastic from the edge of the template and set template aside. Beat sugar and butter in an electric mixer until pale and creamy. Add egg white and beat on lowest speed until incorporated. Add flour and a pinch of salt and mix lightly until combined. Refrigerate for 1 hour to rest (batter will keep refrigerated for 2-3 days).

5 Preheat oven to 180°C. Place template on an oven tray lined with baking paper. Add a teaspoon of the batter into the template and spread the mixture with an offset palette knife so that it fills the template in a thin even layer. Repeat to make 12 tuiles until baking tray is full. Scatter shredded coconut over each and bake until tuiles are golden brown on the edges (8-10 minutes). While still warm, loosen tuiles using a spatula and shape each tuile around a rolling pin, if desired, or cool on tray, then carefully remove. Tuiles will keep in an airtight container for 3 days.

6 To serve, scoop a quenelle of cardamom ice-cream into 6 small dishes and freeze until required. Scatter a thin even layer of extra sugar over each custard. Caramelise with a blowtorch, stand for 5 minutes to crisp, then serve with ice-cream and a tuile, scattered with grated lime zest.

DRINKS MATCH A classic Dark 'n' Stormy cocktail – the ginger beer pairs beautifully with the carrot and cardamom and the rum is the perfect match for the richness of the dish. It's a light and refreshing end to a meal.

Turtle Island

Stow away to an eco-chic private island where crystalline waters and white sandy beaches are met with heartfelt hospitality and the kind of farm-to-table food you won't want to leave behind.

Once discovered, never forgotten. That's the catchcry at Turtle Island. And indeed, a week spent floating through this daydream of a resort etches into the memory bank, shoulders dropping and muscles unfurling in recollection of the stay.

Accessed via seaplane, the family-owned and operated island offers a nurturing brand of luxury. It's a shoe-off, feet-on the shoreline kind of place. And for those seeking replenishment and newly forged memories, it's an ideal destination. It's here, on 200 hectares in the Yasawa Islands, that guests can snorkel, scuba dive, kayak, ride horses or simply melt into their surroundings after a massage at the divine Vonu Spa.

The island's eco-luxe legacy starts with its founder, the late Richard Evanson, who purchased the uninhabited island in 1972, back when it was rendered barren from decades of overgrazing. Evanson arrived with little more than a generator, refrigerator and tent to embark on an extensive reforestation program, eventually planting over half a million trees and rehabilitating the island's natural ecosystems. By 1980 he was ready to open the resort, but not before actress Brooke Shields touched down to film *Blue Lagoon* on this cinematic paradise.

These days, Turtle Island is one of Fiji's longest-running luxury resorts, a hot-ticketed adults-only sanctuary, limited to just 14 couples at a time.

Each of the 14 beachfront bures is gloriously green, with furnishings crafted on-site from fallen trees and driftwood. Over 960 solar panels ensure sustainability, and there's an off-grid romance to the whole stay.

Farm-to-table dining is fuelled by two hectares of vegetable gardens featuring hydroponics and beehives for island honey, while the sublime fresh seafood is either caught by staff or local fishermen. This is just one of the resort's initiatives to support the local community.

There are no traditional restaurants on the island but rather a variety of shared or private dining experiences. Feast in seclusion on one of the 12 private beaches, or a floating pontoon where couples are served by boat, in the famed Blue Lagoon, or at Cliff Point where dinner is served beside a private saltwater pool. Alternatively, join the dinner party at the main table on a beach or mountaintop. Continue the conversation with fellow guests at the beach bar. Naturally, it's all included, down to the top-shelf liquors and guaranteed exclusive-use of a private beach every other day.

Although Turtle Island is typically adults-only, the island welcomes families on selected dates throughout the year. Nature-loving castaways will be quick to return.

EXPLORE

Villas are designed as a guest's
second home with Bure Mamas and
Papas at the ready to guide you
through your Fijian stay. Participate in
catch-to-cook experiences, hike
through Turtle Island's forests or
enjoy a scenic sunrise horseback ride
to arrive at a private beach for a
Champagne breakfast.

Island lobster salad with ginger-lime aïoli and vudi crisps

SERVES 2 // PREP TIME 25 MINS // COOK 25 MINS (PLUS COOLING)

The fresh, sustainable spirit of Turtle Island shines in this salad featuring a mix of locally grown ingredients cultivated in the five-acre vegetable garden. Turtle Island takes pride in using their own sea salt, harvested from the surrounding waters, as well as eggs from the hens and honey from the beehives. The centrepiece is the lobster, responsibly sourced from fishermen on nearby islands. This dish showcases Turtle Island's commitment to freshness and community-supported cuisine.

1   **live rock lobster (400gm) (see note)**
1   **lime, sliced**
35   **gm lettuce (butter or baby cos)**
2   **small heirloom tomatoes, quartered, seeds removed, cut into thin wedges**
½   **small Lebanese cucumber, peeled, cut into julienne**
¼   **small-medium half-ripe papaya (250gm), finely shredded**
  Turtle Island sea salt or other sea salt, to season

VUDI CRISPS
  Vegetable oil, to deep-fry
1   **small vudi (340g), thinly sliced (see note)**

GINGER-LIME AÏOLI
3   **tsp finely grated ginger**
2½   **tbsp lime juice**
1   **egg yolk**
2   **tsp Dijon mustard**
125   **ml vegetable oil**
½   **small garlic clove, finely grated**
2   **tsp Turtle Island honey or other honey**

1 Kill lobster humanely (see note), then remove the head by twisting and pulling the tail and head in opposite directions. Using kitchen scissors, cut down either side of the soft undershell then gently ease out the tail meat. Refrigerate until required.

2 For vudi crisps, heat oil in a deep-fryer or large deep-sided saucepan to 180°C. Deep-fry vudi in batches, stirring frequently until golden and crisp (4-5 minutes). Drain on paper towel and lightly season with sea salt and pepper then set aside.

3 For ginger-lime aïoli, place grated ginger and 2 tbsp lime juice in a small saucepan over low heat and reduce until almost dry (1 minute). Remove from heat. Whisk egg yolk, mustard, salt and pepper to taste in a bowl to combine. Gradually add oil in a thin, steady stream, whisking continuously until thick and emulsified. Whisk in lime and ginger mixture, remaining lime juice, garlic and honey until combined. Season to taste. Makes ¾ cup.

4 To cook the lobster, fill a medium saucepan with water. Add a pinch of salt and 2 slices of lime, and bring the water to a gentle simmer. Do not let the water boil vigorously or it will toughen the lobster meat. Prepare a bowl with iced water. Add the lobster meat to the simmering water and poach until the meat is opaque and tender (4-6 minutes – the cooking time will vary depending on the size of the lobster meat). Poaching lobster meat outside of the shell requires a delicate technique, so ensure the water is at a gentle simmer and watch the lobster meat closely to avoid overcooking it. Using a slotted spoon, transfer lobster meat to the iced water and set aside until cooled, then drain lobster on paper towel. Cut lobster in half lengthways and remove the digestive tract.

5 To serve, arrange lettuce in the centre of two wide bowls and top with tomato and cucumber. Top with a lobster portion placed back into the shell and dress with ginger-lime aïoli. Serve with shredded papaya and vudi crisps.

NOTE RSPCA recommendations for killing crustaceans humanely is to first render the lobster insensible by placing it in the freezer, then inserting a knife into its head to destroy its nerve centre. Vudi is a type of plantain/cooking banana found in Fiji. Substitute with plantain or a large green banana.

MAKE AHEAD Ginger-lime aïoli can be made a day ahead.

DRINKS MATCH Rich, elegant and buttery chardonnays or Mersault-style from Burgundy will work wonderfully with the rich lobster.

Kaikoso clams in lime and soy dressing

SERVES 4 // **PREP TIME 20 MINS**

Handpicked from the pristine shores of the Yasawa Islands, the Kaikoso clam is a delicacy rooted in Fijian culture, where communal efforts in harvesting and sharing the catch underscore the spirit of togetherness. Turtle Island guests are invited to partake in this age-old tradition of clam gathering, an experience that forges a connection with Fijian customs and the ocean. The Kaikoso are returned to the skilled chefs in the kitchen, who transform them into a dish that's both simple and sublime.

160 ml lime juice

160 ml soy sauce

2 tsp finely grated ginger

2 tsp sesame oil

16 large live sashimi-grade clams (Kaikoso, see note)

2 long green chillies, finely diced

2 small heirloom tomatoes, quartered, seeds removed, very thinly sliced

1 spring onion, thinly sliced on the diagonal

1 For dressing, place lime juice, soy sauce, ginger and sesame oil in a small bowl and whisk to combine.

2 Clean the Kaikoso shells thoroughly with a brush under fresh water to remove any debris or sand.

3 To shuck the clams, insert an oyster knife where the two clam shells join, opposite the hinge, then twist the knife gently to pry open. Run the knife along the inside of the shell to cut the abductor muscle which attaches the clam to the shell. Then remove the skirting (outside mantle, this is the slightly frilly band that runs around the outside), preserving the main meat.

4 Rinse the inside of the half shells and reserve the 12 most attractive for serving. Gently return the raw clam meat back into the chosen half shells.

5 Place 4 clams on the half shell on each plate. Drizzle the dressing evenly over the clam meat and garnish with green chilli, tomato and spring onion.

NOTE Kaikoso is a type of local small sweet clam. It's crucial that the clam is sashimi-grade, i.e. extremely fresh if you plan to eat them raw. You could also use other varieties of sashimi-grade clams, or substitute freshly shucked oysters.

DRINKS MATCH Off-dry or semi-sweet styles of riesling with lime-cordial expressions will be a nice counterpoint to the saltiness of the soy while having enough acidity to pair with the clams. Seek out rieslings from New Zealand or Germany.

Kini's chocolate croissants

MAKES 12 // PREP TIME 1 HR (PLUS OVERNIGHT PROVING, STANDING, REFRIGERATION) // COOK 15 MINS

Since 1994, Turtle Island's beloved local Pastry Chef Kini has been delighting guests with her legendary chocolate croissants. Kini's croissants are more than just a breakfast treat; they're a cherished tradition, eagerly anticipated and savoured by those who've made Turtle Island their recurrent getaway. You will need to start this recipe a day ahead.

120 gm Callebaut dark chocolate, cut into
    12 batons
    Icing sugar, to dust (optional)

DANISH PASTRY
125 ml milk, lukewarm
  2 eggs
300 gm bread flour
  5 gm (1½ tsp) dried yeast
1½ tbsp caster sugar
250 gm chilled unsalted butter, chopped

1 For Danish pastry, whisk milk and 1 egg in a medium bowl. Place flour, yeast, 1 tsp fine sea salt and sugar in a food processor, and pulse until combined. Add butter and pulse until butter is chopped into 5mm pieces. Place mixture in a large bowl and stir in milk mixture to form a wet, sticky dough. Cover with plastic wrap and refrigerate overnight.
2 Stand the dough at room temperature for 45 minutes. Place the dough on a well-floured sheet of baking paper and knead lightly. Roll into a 20cm x 50cm rectangle with a floured rolling pin. Fold the dough into thirds by bringing the bottom third over the middle third, then the top third down to cover the folded dough. Turn the dough a quarter turn to the right. Roll into a 20cm x 50cm rectangle again. Repeat folding, turning and rolling twice more, for a total of three times. Cut the dough in half. Wrap each piece in plastic wrap and refrigerate for 30 minutes.
3 To assemble, roll each half of dough into a 20cm x 30cm rectangle. Cut each rectangle into six 10cm squares — you will have 12 squares. Place a chocolate baton in the centre of each square piece. Fold the pastry over the chocolate to create a triangle, then roll up starting from the wide base (see notes). Line two large oven trays with baking paper. Place pastries 5cm apart on the prepared trays and cover loosely with oiled plastic wrap. Stand in a warm place for 30 minutes.
4 Meanwhile, preheat oven to 180°C and line two large oven trays with baking paper. For eggwash, beat remaining egg in a small bowl until smooth then set aside. Brush pastries with eggwash then bake until puffed and golden (16-20 minutes).
5 Cool the chocolate croissants for a few minutes before serving warm, dusted with icing sugar, if using.

NOTE Alternatively, if you want to form these into a simpler shape, fold the two opposite pastry corners to meet in the centre and press together, then continue with the recipe.

DRINKS MATCH For the holiday goers who would like an early morning libation or a boozy brunch at home, nothing pairs as wonderfully with a chocolate fuelled breakfast pastry as syrupy sweet botrytis Semillon, low in alcohol but packed with golden flavours to pair with the flaky pastry.

Jean-Michel Cousteau Resort

Pristine above the water's surface and spectacular below it. Eco-luxe families will revel in an environmentally and culturally oriented resort that redirects the power of Fiji's tourism lure for good.

People will protect what they love. This is sustainability gospel according to French environmentalist and oceanographic explorer Jean-Michel Cousteau. For years, the marine conservationist (son of another world-famous ocean adventurer, Jacques Cousteau) put his theory into practice through documentary and philanthropy. Perhaps his greatest interrogation into the philosophy is at the resort he founded in 1995, located in Savusavu on the northern tip of Vanua Levu, Fiji's second largest island. By creating the prototypical luxury eco resort, Cousteau set out to prove the business case for sustainable tourism. And by stirring up adoration for natural playgrounds above and below the waters' surface, the resort deftly turns guests into conservationists-in-waiting.

Follow the scuba aficionados to Cousteau Dive Centre, where first-timers can learn to dive in the coral-filled waters around the resort, or head out to the world-famous Namena Marine Reserve, just a short boat ride from the resort's sandy shores. Here you'll find coral-reef scenes that seem to be cut from *Finding Nemo* (coincidentally, Cousteau makes an animated appearance in the film's DVD release).

While adults dive, children can have their own marine educational experience in The School Under the Sea. This is part of the Bula Club for Kids, complete with water slides, a paddling pool, trampoline and lessons with a resident marine biologist. All young children are assigned a dedicated nanny for the duration of their stay, while older kids (between six to 12) are gathered into groups of five and led by a buddy for playtime and kids' meals.

With the younger generation otherwise engaged, parents are freed up for the occasional child-free meal under moonlight at the end of a pier or on the beach.

Dining is à la carte and farm-to-table, with tropical flavours grown in the organic gardens. What the resort doesn't grow it sustainably sources from nearby farms and the surrounding ocean. This is in an effort to minimise food miles and nurture the local economy, in line with the resort's foundational belief that modern society can learn a lot from Fijian agricultural and fishing traditions.

Guests who choose to keep the cultural learnings coming can join guided excursions to a nearby village (bring a gift, known as sevusevu, to ingratiate yourself to the villagers) or learn to weave palm crafts like a local.

Designed to reflect Fijian architecture, the guest bures are also deeply rooted in a sense of place. And the same is true of the spa's beachside treatment bures and yoga pavilions. The result is a holiday that imprints a piece of Fiji on the soul so that departing guests leave this haven a little wiser, more relaxed and far greener.

EXPLORE

Head out on a "Day of Ecological Awareness" Eco Walk, joining one of the resident marine biologists to discover sustainable initiatives championed by Jean-Michel Cousteau Resort. Here, you'll experience traditional Fijian botanical wellness medicines known as "Wai Vakaviti" grown in the organic farm.

Blackened snapper with cucumber salad

SERVES 2 // PREP TIME 20 MINS (PLUS MARINTATING) // COOK 10 MINS

"[This is] a canvas of scored Fiji snapper fillets adorned with the bold contrasting flavours of miso," says Chef Gerard Marr. "Searing to perfection yields a crisp skin, while the fillets rest gracefully beside a refreshing salad of home-grown fragrant herbs and ribbons of cucumber. It's a pairing of richness and vibrant simplicity."

2 Pakapaka or snapper fillets (180-200gm each), skin on (see note)
2 tbsp shiro (white) miso paste
1 tbsp soy sauce
2 tbsp mirin
1½ tbsp vegetable oil
Lemon wedges, to serve

CUCUMBER SALAD
1 medium Lebanese cucumber
¼ cup each of mint, basil, coriander, dill leaves and sprigs
Juice of 1 lemon
2 garlic cloves, finely chopped

1 Using a sharp knife, make three shallow diagonal cuts into fish skin and pat skin dry. Line a plate with baking paper and place fish on the plate, skin-side down.

2 Combine miso, soy sauce and mirin in a small bowl. Brush miso mixture onto the flesh side of the fish only, cover and refrigerate to marinate (minimum 1 hour or ideally up to 4 hours).

3 Preheat oven to 150°C. Heat little oil in a non-stick, ovenproof frying pan over medium heat. Sear fish, skin-side down, until skin is crisp (4-5 minutes). Turn fish over then transfer to the oven to finish cooking (3-4 minutes).

4 Meanwhile, for cucumber salad, using a vegetable peeler (or mandoline), peel cucumber into ribbons, then add to a bowl with remaining ingredients. Season to taste and toss gently to combine.

5 Divide cucumber salad and fish among plates. Drizzle with the liquid from the cucumber salad and serve with lemon wedges.

NOTE Pakapaka (crimson jobfish, deepwater snapper, pink snapper) is from the lutjanidae (tropical snapper) family; substitute with other firm white-fleshed fish.

DRINKS MATCH The red fruits in both a French beaujolais or a lighter-style grenache would pair wonderfully with the salty and smoky characters in the miso-blackened fish. Don't forget to refrigerate them before you drink to get the most vibrancy out of the wines.

Lemongrass prawn skewers with Thai green curry cappuccino

SERVES 6 // PREP TIME 45 MINS (PLUS MARINATING) // COOK 1 HR (PLUS INFUSING)

"A tropical infusion of succulent prawns, marinated in vibrant herb green curry, threaded on lemongrass stems, and grilled to perfection," says Chef Gerard Marr. "Paired with a fragrant green curry cappuccino, this dish is a modern ode to the resort's organic farm, inviting guests to savour the harmony of spiced herbs and seafood sweetness."

Freeze-dried makrut lime powder, coriander leaves and makrut lime leaves, to serve

GREEN CURRY PASTE
- 6 **long green chillies, seeds removed**
- 5 **cm piece galangal, peeled, chopped**
- 2 **lemongrass stalks, white part only**
- 6 **makrut lime leaves, plus extra, to serve**
- 2 **shallots or 1 small onion**
- 6 **garlic cloves**
- 2 **tsp shrimp paste (belacan, see note), roasted**
- 2 **tsp lime zest**
- ¼ **cup coriander leaves**
- 2 **tbsp chopped coriander roots (see note), rinsed and scraped**

LEMONGRASS PRAWN SKEWERS
- 1 **tbsp green curry paste (recipe above)**
- 1 **tbsp fish sauce**
- 12 **large raw prawns (60gm), peeled and deveined**
- 6 **thin lemongrass stalks, cut into 15cm lengths for skewers (see notes)**
- 1 **tbsp fish sauce**

GREEN CURRY CAPPUCCINO
- 750 **ml coconut cream**
- 1½ **tbsp green curry paste (recipe above)**
- 250 **ml prawn or seafood stock**
- 60 **ml fish sauce**
- 1 **tbsp lemon or lime juice**
- 2 **tbsp grated light palm sugar**
- 1 **lemongrass stalk, bruised**
- 2 **makrut lime leaves**

1 For green curry paste, coarsely chop chillies, then finely chop galangal, lemongrass, makrut lime leaves, shallot and garlic, keeping each ingredient separate. Using a mortar and pestle, pound the chillies and then add each paste ingredient separately, from hardest to softest. Pound to a pulp before adding the next ingredient until a fine paste forms. Makes ¾ cup.

2 For lemongrass prawn skewers, combine 1 tbsp green curry paste and fish sauce in a bowl. Add prawns and turn to coat, then refrigerate for flavours to infuse (15-20 minutes). Skewer two prawns onto each lemongrass skewer.

3 Meanwhile, for green curry cappuccino, place 125ml coconut cream in a medium saucepan over medium heat. Cook until cream separates and becomes oily, then add green curry paste. Cook, stirring, until fragrant (3-4 minutes). Add stock and 375ml coconut cream and bring to a simmer. Cook gently for flavours to infuse (15-20 minutes), then season with fish sauce, lemon juice and sugar. For infused coconut cream, place remaining 250ml coconut cream in a second saucepan. Add lemongrass and lime leaves, crushing the leaves in your palm as you add them to the pan. Heat over low heat for flavours to infuse (10 minutes). Set aside and discard lemongrass and lime leaves.

4 Heat a greased barbecue or char-grill pan to high. Grill lemongrass prawn skewers, turning, until cooked through (2-3 minutes each side).

5 To serve, ladle green curry cappuccino base among bowls. Using a stick blender, froth infused coconut cream and pour over the base liquid, then dust with makrut lime powder. Add a prawn skewer and garnish with coriander and a makrut lime leaf.

NOTE Belacan is a shrimp paste available from Asian grocers. To roast, preheat oven to 180°C, wrap belacan in foil and roast (10-15 minutes). Alternatively, because the belacan becomes very pungent during roasting, you can roast it outside on an enclosed barbecue. You will need 8 coriander roots, wash then scrape the outsides to clean. You can also use bamboo skewers, soak them in boiling water for 10 minutes then dry them before using.

DRINKS MATCH With lemongrass being such a dominant flavour in this dish, it will work cohesively with white wines that display this character – think sauvignon blanc and riesling.

White chocolate passionfruit mousse with coconut caramel sauce

SERVES 8 // PREP TIME 40 MINS (PLUS SETTING) // COOK 15 MINS (PLUS COOLING)

"A dance of sweetness, balanced with fresh creamy coconut and capturing the essence of caramelised richness," says Chef Gerard Marr. "Indulgent white chocolate pairs with tropical passionfruit in this creamy mousse with contrasting coconut caramel crunch."

Edible flowers, to serve

**WHITE CHOCOLATE
PASSIONFRUIT MOUSSE**

260 gm white couverture chocolate, chopped
3 egg yolks
55 gm caster sugar
50 ml milk
10 gm powdered gelatine
500 ml pouring cream
250 ml passionfruit pulp (about 8 passionfruit), plus extra to serve
Micro mint, to serve

COCONUT TOFFEE
75 gm light palm sugar, finely grated
150 gm fresh grated coconut (see note)

COCONUT CARAMEL SAUCE
200 gm brown sugar
400 ml coconut cream
Sea salt flakes, to taste

1 For white chocolate passionfruit mousse, place chocolate in a heatproof bowl over a saucepan of gently simmering water, until chocolate just melts. Remove bowl from the water and set aside to cool.

2 Meanwhile, place egg yolks and sugar in the bowl of an electric mixer with the whisk attachment and whisk until thick and pale. Gently fold melted chocolate into egg yolk mixture. Place milk in a small heatproof bowl, then sprinkle gelatine over. Place bowl in a saucepan of gently simmering water and stir until dissolved.

3 In a clean bowl, whisk cream until medium peaks form. Add milk and gelatine mixture to the chocolate mixture, then fold in whipped cream and passionfruit pulp. Pour mixture into 1.5 litre 9cm x 27cm (6cm deep) loaf pan, then refrigerate to set (4-6 hours).

4 For coconut toffee, sprinkle palm sugar evenly across the base of a medium frying pan. Place over medium-heat and watch the sugar carefully and wait until it starts to melt. Simmer until amber golden (3-5 minutes), then stir in the coconut. Spread onto a baking-paper-lined oven tray then leave to cool (30 minutes).

5 For coconut caramel sauce, sprinkle the brown sugar evenly across the base of a large frying pan. Place over medium-high heat and watch the sugar carefully. Stir it a little to make sure the bottom doesn't burn before the top has melted. When it starts to melt and caramelise, immediately stir through coconut cream (take care as the caramel will bubble quickly). Pass through a fine sieve and sprinkle with salt when cooled. Makes 1½ cups.

6 To serve, spoon caramel sauce on plates then top with a quenelle of mousse and coconut toffee. Drizzle with extra passionfruit pulp and serve with mint.

NOTE If you can't get fresh coconut, substitute with desiccated coconut.

DRINKS MATCH So many delicate and floral driven flavours calls for a light and aromatic wine to match, an Italian Moscato d'Asti will be the perfect pairing with its own floral notes and delicate bubble to enhance the dessert.

Vatuvara Private Islands

Conscientious luxury comes to Kaibu Island in the picture-perfect Northern Lau Group. This is home to an all-inclusive Fijian fantasy resort that cares for the planet as it nurtures the soul.

Sustainability, in traditional and state-of-the-art forms, weaves through this top-tier adults-only resort to make paradise even more pristine. Glorious as the luxury setting is, it's made that much lovelier by the sense your lavish holiday is doing good by humanity and the planet.

This carbon-negative destination, powered by Tesla solar energy and fuelled by the organic farm, proves how conservation and tourism can unite to support scientific research and community development. In partnership with the Vatuvara Foundation, the resort practices what they call "Ridge to Reef" conservation, protecting the marine environment through coral nurseries and repopulation. Dive or snorkel in the kaleidoscopic coral reef, warmed by the knowledge your adventure is helping to support biodiversity among thousands of marine life species. There is stunning snorkelling to be experienced just footsteps from the resort, or take a boat to one of the premier dive sites in the untouched natural reserve where you might spot an endangered coconut crab, threatened giant clams or a hawksbill sea turtle.

Accessed only by the resort's Twin Otter aircraft, from either Suva or Nadi, the 320-hectare all-inclusive haven is home to just three meticulous villas, each one expansive, all with private beach access and including bionised infinity edge plunge pools, plus massage bures with personal masseuses on standby.

The high standards of the guest spaces carry through to the dining in two seaside full-service restaurants. Jim's Bar and Grill is the casual go-to for beachside breakfast and lunches, featuring smoothies, salads, woodfired pizzas, and baked goods served with homemade jams and preserves. Then at night, Valhalla is the place for dinner and drinks, perched above the lapping waters of the South Pacific. Here, sleek bites are paired with fine wines and liquors from the formidable cellar.

Ingredients are all as fresh as can be, either grown on the island (the garden is leading the way in climate-resilient crop cultivation) or sustainably caught in the surrounding ocean, safeguarding the future food bowl for the whole island from the realities of climate change.

Feast on modern Pacific Rim cuisine, or better yet, take part in a cooking lesson to learn the nuances of local dishes from the chefs who proudly share their family recipes.

Cooking classes, dining, wine and private air transfers are all included in the nightly rate. So too are the Champagne picnics and just about anything the heart desires, which makes doing right by the world a tantalising prospect.

EXPLORE

Discover the lagoon and fringing reef by SUP or kayak or don a snorkel and swim out from the shore to encounter the resort's coral restoration nurseries, giant clam, sea turtles, spotted eagle rays, reef sharks and tropical fish among vibrant corals.

Fish and prawn island sliders

SERVES 8 // PREP TIME 45 MINS (PLUS PROVING) // COOK 35 MINS

Experience the freshness of an authentic ocean-to-table meal with fish and prawns coated in an airy batter, layered in fluffy buns made with mashed potato and milk. These sliders are rounded out with a zippy dressing.

400	gm firm white fish, cut into wide strips
480	gm raw prawns or lobster tails, peeled, deveined
8	baby cos lettuce leaves
1	bulb baby fennel, shaved on a mandoline

POTATO BUNS

525	gm plain flour
1¼	tsp fine sea salt
2	tsp instant dried yeast
115	gm mashed potato
310	ml milk, plus extra to brush
1	tbsp vegetable oil
1	tsp sesame seeds

MANY ISLANDS DRESSING

200	gm mayonnaise
1	tbsp sriracha (Thai hot chilli sauce), or to taste
1	tbsp tomato ketchup
1	tbsp gherkin relish or finely chopped cornichons (sour gherkins)

TEMPURA BATTER

150	gm plain flour, plus extra to dust
75	gm cornflour
330	ml can soda water
1	cup ice cubes
	Vegetable oil, to deep-fry

1 For potato bun dough, place flour, salt and yeast in the bowl of an electric mixer and stir with a whisk. Combine mashed potato, milk and vegetable oil in a jug until smooth. Add wet ingredients to dry ingredients and, using an electric mixer fitted with a dough hook, mix until a smooth dough forms (5 minutes). Transfer to a greased bowl, cover with a clean towel and let prove in a warm place until doubled in size (1½ hours).

2 To shape and cook potato buns, turn dough out onto a lightly floured surface, gently punch down, then divide into eight (110g each) pieces. Roll each piece into a 6cm ball, then place 8cm apart on a large baking-paper-lined oven tray. Cover with a clean towel and prove on the tray until doubled in size (1 hour). Towards the end of rising, preheat oven to 180°C. Brush the tops of the buns with a little extra milk and sprinkle with sesame seeds. Bake buns until risen and lightly golden (15-20 minutes), then transfer to a wire rack to cool. Store cooled buns in an airtight container for up to 2 days.

3 For Many Islands dressing, combine ingredients in a small bowl, then season, adjusting with more sriracha to taste.

4 For tempura batter, sift flours into a bowl. Combine soda water and ice in a jug, pour over flour mixture and mix to form a lumpy batter the consistency of pouring cream.

5 To cook tempura seafood, heat vegetable oil in a large deep saucepan or deep-fryer to 180°C. Dust fish and prawns in flour then dip, one at a time, into batter. Deep-fry, turning halfway, until lightly golden and crisp (1-2 minutes). Drain on paper towel.

6 To assemble, cut buns in half horizontally. In batches, toast cut-sides of potato buns in a heated oiled frying pan (30 seconds -1 minute). Spread bun bases with a little dressing, then layer with lettuce and shaved fennel. Drizzle with a little more dressing, then top with tempura seafood and cap with bun lid. Secure with a skewer.

NOTE For a light tempura batter, be careful not to overmix or you will activate the gluten in the flour.

DRINKS MATCH A dry style of sparkling wine will cut through the richness of the tempura fish and the buttery bread, think Vintage Australian sparkling or a classic style of Champagne.

Lobster salad with steamed potatoes and lemon vinaigrette

SERVES 4 // PREP TIME 30 MINS (PLUS FREEZING) // COOK 15 MINS (PLUS COOLING)

For this recipe the Vatuvara chefs use mana, a local mangrove lobster; *Thalassina anomala*. The meat is sweet and delicate, and pairs well with the bitter leaves and herbs, sourced from the island farm.

2   live mud lobsters
    (about 900gm each, see note)
400 gm kipfler potatoes,
    scrubbed
200 gm sugarsnap peas or snow peas,
    halved
1   small radicchio, leaves separated
1   white witlof, leaves separated
2   baby cucumbers, thinly
    sliced lengthways
    Micro lemon balm, to serve

LEMON VINAIGRETTE
60 ml lemon juice
1   garlic clove, finely grated on
    a microplane
1   tsp Dijon mustard
¼   tsp sea salt
½   tsp honey
½   tsp finely chopped thyme
60 ml extra-virgin olive oil

1 Kill lobsters humanely (see note). Cover and refrigerate until required.

2 Bring a large saucepan or stockpot of heavily salted water to the boil over medium-high heat. Add lobsters and cook until flesh is just set (8 minutes). Drain, then refresh immediately in a large bowl of iced water. Working with one lobster at a time, remove head by twisting and pulling the tail and head in opposite directions, discard head. Using kitchen scissors, cut down either side of the under shell, then gently ease out tail meat and remove digestive tract. Repeat with second lobster. Refrigerate until required.

3 For lemon vinaigrette, place all ingredients except olive oil in a bowl and whisk until salt dissolves. Gradually whisk in olive oil until emulsified. Season to taste.

4 Place potatoes in a saucepan and cover with cold water. Bring to the boil over high heat and cook until tender (10 minutes). Drain, and when cooled, cut into rounds. Place potato slices in a bowl, add 2 tbsp of vinaigrette and toss gently to coat.

5 Blanch sugarsnap peas in a saucepan of salted water until just tender (30 seconds). Drain then plunge immediately into a bowl of iced water to cool, then drain.

6 Cut cooked lobster into thick slices. Place sugarsnap peas, radicchio and witlof in a bowl, drizzle with 60ml dressing and toss gently to combine.

7 Arrange dressed salad, potato, cucumber and lobster on four plates. Garnish with micro lemon balm and drizzle with a little more dressing to serve.

NOTE Mud lobsters, like rock lobsters, contain the bulk of their meat in the body, with non-existent meat in their claws. If unavailable, substitute mud lobster with rock lobster, scampi, or large prawns. RSPCA recommendations for killing crustaceans humanely is to first render the lobster insensible by placing it in the freezer, then inserting a knife into its head to destroy its nerve centre.

MAKE AHEAD Lemon vinaigrette can be made a day ahead.

DRINKS MATCH A chilled modern-style Australian chardonnay will pair beautifully with every element in this dish – minerality for the crayfish, buttery top notes for the potatoes and lemon acidity to finish.

Citrus hibiscus granita and coconut ice-cream

SERVES 8 // PREP TIME 30 MINS (PLUS INFUSING AND OVERNIGHT FREEZING) // COOK 30 MINS

"All our ingredients are sourced locally or grown on-site," says Executive Chef Wendy King. "We use fresh deep-red hibiscus from our gardens, however in order to make this recipe accessible for wherever you live we have adapted it to use candied hibiscus in syrup. It's just as refreshing to add to the lemongrass-spiked granita, perfect after a day in the sun."

CITRUS HIBISCUS GRANITA

- 75 gm caster sugar
- 1 stalk lemongrass (white part only), thinly sliced
- 3 cm ginger (15g), grated
- 250 gm jar wild hibiscus flowers in syrup (see note)
- 2 tbsp lemon juice
- 2 finger limes and micro lemon balm (optional), to serve

COCONUT ICE-CREAM

- 1 litre milk
- 200 gm desiccated coconut
- 500 ml pouring cream
- 8 egg yolks
- 200 gm caster sugar

1 For granita, bring 400ml water, sugar, lemongrass and ginger to the boil in a saucepan over medium heat, stirring to dissolve sugar. Remove from heat and set aside to infuse (30 minutes).

2 Meanwhile, strain hibiscus syrup and flowers from the jar into a bowl, reserving candied flowers. Stir lemon juice into hibiscus syrup, then strain lemongrass and ginger syrup into the bowl with hibiscus syrup and combine well. Discard solids.

3 Pour syrup mixture into a 22cm square shallow tin pan and place in the freezer until mixture is frozen (overnight). A few hours before serving, scrape the frozen mixture in the pan with a fork to form ice crystals, then return to the freezer until ready to serve.

4 For coconut ice-cream, place milk, coconut and 375ml of the cream in a large saucepan and bring to just below boiling point, then set aside to infuse (1 hour). Meanwhile, whisk egg yolks with sugar until pale and creamy, then add milk mixture and whisk to combine well. Strain through a coarse sieve into a clean saucepan, pressing down firmly on solids to remove all liquid. Stir over low-medium heat until mixture thickens enough to coat the back of the spoon (8-12 minutes). Transfer to a bowl placed over ice, add remaining cream and stir for 2 minutes, then stand until chilled. Churn in an ice-cream machine, following manufacturer's instructions, then transfer to a container, cover and freeze until required.

5 To serve, scoop ice-cream into chilled wide bowls, then spoon granita around. Serve immediately garnished with reserved candied hibiscus flowers, finger limes and micro lemon balm, if using.

NOTE Wild hibiscus flower in syrup is available from select delicatessens and liquor stores.

MAKE AHEAD Granita can be made up to 3 days ahead, re-scrape with a fork when ready to serve.

DRINKS MATCH A classic Kir Royale cocktail – the black raspberry liqueur will bring out the hibiscus notes, while the sparkling wine keeps everything fresh so as not to overpower this delicate dessert.

Yasawa Island Resort & Spa

Six Fijian villages, 11 private beaches and just one place to stay on the island. Step ashore at this exclusive resort for adults-only resplendence or during the designated family times for azure-tinged shared memories.

You can lose hours watching the tides change from the palm-strung hammock fronting your secluded Pacific-chic bungalow. The clock has a way of losing significance here, far removed from television and traffic. This is Fiji time at its best, made more languid by a procession of eye-candy moments such as the cinnamon wood pergolas and rattan pendants to captivate the gaze. The weather plays its part too in making schedules fade into the ether. Located at the very top of the Yasawa Island Group, Yasawa Island is in the sunniest and driest part of Fiji, basking in truly lavish tropical climes and warm ocean temperatures all year round. Even in the wet season (November to April), this corner of Fiji experiences the country's lowest rainfall levels.

Take stock in the bungalows. There are just 18 of them scattered around the resort on this 2800-hectare island. Each one is outfitted to impress, after a six-month, million-dollar refurbishment, which was completed in March 2024. Beyond the revamped guest bures, the large-scale overhaul also ushered in an updated beachfront bar, restaurant, wine room and library, with each new or improved area blending style with sustainability.

Yasawa is one of the many Fijian words for heaven, and the exclusive resort doesn't over promise or under deliver. It's the only resort on an island that is framed by 11 beaches. And the only neighbours on the landform are the locals who reside in the six villages. Connect with the customs of the land and sea, as Yasawa Island locals generously open up their lives to visitors. Take part in a traditional meke (Fijian singing and dancing event). Share kava with elders or listen to the choir on a Sunday from the beach. These are the moments that make this slice of Fiji far more meaningful than just any other beach break.

Your cultural education continues in the alfresco restaurant. Dine on lobster, crab and seared tuna caught fresh by village fishermen, enjoying a taste of Fiji alongside incredible views overlooking the pool, beach and ocean. Then head to Manasa's Bar where head bartender Manasa shakes up tropical cocktails to enjoy from the deck.

Yasawa Island Resort is all-inclusive (barring alcohol) and adults-only (except during designated family times). It's a 35-minute scenic flight from Nadi to get to the island, which is included in the stay. And if you can ply yourself away from the hammock or the sun-kissed beaches for a while, a visit to the spa or a private picnic on a secluded beach is good use of all that elastic time.

EXPLORE

Head out into the Yasawa Island chain to swim in the famous Blue Lagoon Caves, or remain on Yasawa Island to meet the Chief or visit the local village of Bukama, stopping by the traditional shell market.

Seared tuna with Fijian-style potato curry

SERVES 4 // PREP TIME 20 MINS (PLUS QUICK PICKLING) // COOK 30 MINS (PLUS RESTING)

"We use sustainably sourced Fijian tuna direct from the waters off Yasawa, potatoes from the local Bukama village and a hit of Fijian Bongo chillies for the extra hint of spice," says owner James McCann.

800	gm potatoes (see note), peeled, cut into 4cm pieces
80	gm ghee
1	medium red onion (170 gm), finely chopped
1	Bongo (Habanero) chilli, seeds removed, finely chopped, plus extra to serve
2	cm piece ginger, finely grated
1	garlic clove, crushed
1	tsp mild curry powder
1	tsp ground turmeric
3	tsp brown mustard seeds
½	tsp chilli powder
10	fresh curry leaves, plus extra fried leaves (see note), to serve
½	tsp caster sugar
4	tuna steaks (180gm each)
½	cup (loosely packed) coriander leaves

RED ONION PICKLE

60	ml rice vinegar
1	tsp caster sugar
1	small red onion (80gm), thinly sliced into rounds

1 Place potato in a saucepan of cold salted water and bring to the boil over high heat. Cook until par-cooked (5 minutes). Drain.

2 Meanwhile, for red onion pickle, combine vinegar, sugar and ½ tsp sea salt in a small bowl, stirring until sugar dissolves. Add red onion and toss to combine, then set aside until required.

3 Heat 40gm of the ghee in a frying pan over medium heat. Add onion and cook, stirring, until soft (2-3 minutes). Add chilli, ginger, garlic and dry spices, and cook, stirring, for a further 1 minute or until fragrant. Add cooked potato to the pan, along with curry leaves and 250ml water. Cover and cook, shaking the pan frequently to prevent the potato catching on the base (10 minutes). Remove the lid, add remaining ghee and cook, uncovered, stirring occasionally, until potato begins to crisp (5 minutes). Remove from the heat, stir in sugar and season, then set aside to keep warm.

4 Meanwhile, heat a char-grill pan or barbecue to high. Season tuna and grill for 1 minute each side or until seared but still rare in the centre. Transfer tuna to a tray and rest loosely covered with foil (5 minutes).

5 Drain red onion, reserving some liquid for serving. Return to the bowl with coriander leaves and toss to combine. Season.

6 Divide potato curry and tuna among plates. Top with red onion pickle, coriander, extra chilli and fried curry leaves. Drizzle with a little reserved pickling liquid to serve.

NOTE Use a good all-rounder style of potato, like sebago or desiree, that will hold its shape well during cooking. To fry curry leaves, heat 2 tbsp olive or vegetable oil in a small frying pan. Add curry leaves and cook until they stop sizzling (30 seconds-1 minute), then transfer to a plate lined with paper towel.

DRINKS MATCH There are a lot of earthy elements in this dish along with the slight char on the tuna from searing. A lightly chilled dolcetto from Italy, with its bright-red fruit notes, will create a nice counter-balance to this dish.

Yasawa gazpacho

SERVES 4 // PREP TIME 25 MINS (PLUS REFRIGERATION) // COOK 10 MINS

"This is our Fijian version of a classic recipe, perfect for the tropical climate – a cool, refreshing mix of freshly sourced local organic produce balanced with wild Fijian lemongrass, chilled and served with crisp croûtons," says owner James McCann.

Toasted flaked almonds and small basil leaves, to serve

GAZPACHO
1 kg ripe heirloom tomatoes, chopped
1 small red onion (80g), finely chopped
1 Lebanese cucumber, peeled, seeds removed, chopped
1 red or green capsicum, chopped
2 celery stalks, chopped
1 stalk lemongrass (white part only), finely chopped
1-2 tbsp chopped flat-leaf parsley
2 tbsp chopped chives
1 garlic clove, finely chopped
600 ml tomato juice or 400gm can crushed tomatoes
60 ml red wine vinegar
60 ml extra-virgin olive oil, plus extra, to serve
1 tbsp lemon juice
1 tsp caster sugar, or to taste
6 drops Tabasco sauce, or to taste

CROÛTONS
100 gm day-old rustic-style bread, crusts removed, cut into 1cm cubes
1 garlic clove, bruised
60 ml extra-virgin olive oil

1 For gazpacho, place ingredients in a large bowl. Using a stick blender, blend until smooth with a little bit of texture.

2 Season with sea salt and pepper, then adjust the seasoning to taste with more salt, pepper, sugar and Tabasco. Transfer to an airtight container and refrigerate for several hours to chill and for flavours to develop.

3 Meanwhile, for croûtons, place bread and garlic in a bowl, drizzle with olive oil and season to taste, then toss well to coat. Spread out on a small oven tray lined with baking paper and bake, turning occasionally, until golden (8-10 minutes). Discard garlic and set aside to cool.

4 To serve, ladle soup into bowls, scatter with croûtons, then garnish with flaked almonds and basil leaves. Drizzle with extra olive oil.

DRINKS MATCH Keep your wine choices light and zippy, much like the dish – sparkling rosé would be an excellent idea.

Rich chocolate terrine with chocolate sponge and rum topping

SERVES 18 // PREP TIME 45 MINS // COOK 30 MINS (PLUS COOLING, FREEZING, REFRIGERATION)

"Pure single origin Fijian cacao chocolate is the key to our decadent chocolate terrine, which is complemented with handcrafted Fijian Ratu spiced rum for a unique twist to a favourite dessert," says owner James McCann.

Crème fraîche, chocolate shapes and raspberries, to serve

CHOCOLATE SPONGE

175 gm unsalted butter, at room temperature
175 gm golden caster sugar
3 eggs
100 gm self-raising flour
50 gm Fijian cocoa powder
40 ml milk

CHOCOLATE TERRINE

800 ml pouring cream
800 gm Fijian milk chocolate, finely chopped
400 gm Fijian dark chocolate (72%), finely chopped
4 egg yolks
250 gm unsalted butter, at room temperature

CHOCOLATE RUM TOPPING

300 gm Fijian dark chocolate (72%), chopped
50 ml Ratu spiced rum (see note)
60 ml pouring cream

1 For chocolate sponge, preheat oven to 180°C. Grease a 23cm x 33.5cm (6cm deep) cake tin, then line base with baking paper. Beat butter and sugar with an electric mixer until light and fluffy. Beat in eggs one at a time until incorporated. Fold in combined sifted flour and cocoa, alternating with milk until combined. Spoon into prepared tin and level. Bake until a skewer inserted into the centre comes out clean (18-20 minutes). Stand cake in tin for 5 minutes before inverting onto a wire rack to cool. Once cool, transfer to an airtight container until required.

2 For chocolate terrine, wash and dry same cake tin used to cook sponge. Grease and line base and sides of tin with baking paper, extending paper 5cm beyond tin rim. Place cream in a large saucepan and bring to just below boiling point. Place chocolates in a heatproof bowl, then pour hot cream over. Stand for 3 minutes, then whisk until melted and combined. Whisk in egg yolks one at a time until incorporated, then gradually whisk in butter until incorporated.

3 Return chocolate sponge to prepared tin, base-side up, pressing gently to ensure cake is level. Pour over chocolate terrine layer and level. Freeze until set (4 hours or overnight).

4 For chocolate rum topping, place chocolate in a bowl and melt over a saucepan of gently simmering water. Remove bowl from pan and stir in rum and cream until combined. Set aside 60ml for serving. Remove terrine from freezer, pour chocolate rum layer over terrine filling, then quickly spread to cover evenly. Refrigerate to set (30 minutes).

5 To serve, using paper as an aid, carefully lift terrine from tin. Using a knife dipped in hot water then dried each time, cut terrine into eighteen 3cm x 6cm rectangles. Place terrine on plates, then decorate plates with reserved chocolate rum topping, a quenelle of crème fraîche, chocolate shapes and raspberries.

NOTE Fiji Ratu spiced rum is aged in charred oak barrels, filtered through coconut shell carbon, and is flavoured with vanilla, orange, cinnamon and star anise. You can substitute with other spiced rum.

MAKE AHEAD Terrine can be assembled up to 2 days ahead. Chocolate sponge can be made a day ahead of assembly. Terrine will keep in the freezer for up to 1 month; transfer to the fridge 4 hours before serving and serve semifreddo.

DRINKS MATCH The layers of chocolate in all their glory needs a wine with its own opulent flavours. Enter a plush, red-fruited sparkling shiraz.

SARAH FARAG

Owner and director, Southern Crossings New Zealand

Sarah Farag was only three years of age when she first visited the islands of Fiji. It was then also that her lifelong friendship with these beautiful isles began; their genuine warmth inviting frequent visits in the decades that followed. The idyllic islands of Fiji have provided the backdrop for many happy memories: from childhood family holidays and a romantic tropical honeymoon to several wonderful trips with her own children and extended family.

Over these many visits to Fiji, Sarah has had the privilege of travelling to more than 20 fabulous resorts across the island nation, discovering many of its most celebrated travel experiences and uncovering countless hidden treasures: experiences and insights that she and her astute team of Travel Designers now also share with discerning travellers from around the globe to curate truly personalised tropical island holidays. The welcoming destination has become a natural extension to her luxury travel business in New Zealand.

Owner and Director of Southern Crossings New Zealand, Sarah's extensive luxury travel expertise and local connections have earned her place on a collection of coveted international travel lists including *Condé Nast Traveler*'s list of the world's leading travel specialists, *Town & Country*'s list of travel gurus, Wendy Perrin's WOW List and *Travel + Leisure*'s A-List.

Spend any time with Sarah and her passion for travel, her dedication to delivering "above and beyond" experiences and her ability to connect people and places are immediately clear — and are echoed throughout her talented travel team as Southern Crossings now celebrates over 38 years of designing industry-leading New Zealand, Australia and Fiji luxury travel experiences.

southern-crossings.com

Acknowledgements

Having already partnered with *Gourmet Traveller* on two beautiful coffee table books showcasing Australia and New Zealand; and with Fiji's largely untold food story enjoying a wonderful evolution in recent years, it's apt to share the luxury travel experiences that flavour Southern Crossings' curated journeys across the South Pacific islands of Fiji.

As Southern Crossings celebrates nearly four decades of sharing New Zealand, Australia and the South Pacific's finest destinations with sophisticated travellers from around the globe, we are delighted to share this collection of delectable Fijian temptations.

With its rich melting pot of multicultural influences and abundance of fresh local produce, Fijian cuisine celebrates a vibrant local culture. Traditional shared feasts and romantic beach picnics enjoyed in spectacular tropical settings deliver some of the destination's most memorable travel experiences. It is therefore our intention with this book to share some of Fiji's most amazing experiences through the culinary experiences they offer.

Our heartfelt thanks go to the many people and partners who have brought this project to life:

To all of the very special properties featured in these pages who not only inspired this book, but also opened their kitchens and shared their stories, and who helped make this book possible.

To caterers Komal and Sonali Swamy of Koko & Chai who shared their passion for modern Fijian flavours from their Auckland-based kitchen.

To Tourism Fiji, for their kind support that has helped us to tell Fiji's exceptional food narratives and share the destination's most inviting luxury travel experiences.

To the *Gourmet Traveller* team who have again so beautifully brought our vision to life.

To my fellow Southern Crossings directors and the entire Southern Crossings team, including the Travel Designers who passionately curate Fiji's most rewarding experiences with a dedication that only comes from a genuine love of what they do, and for which I am truly grateful every day.

And to our collaborators, Bettina Kramer, Sara Devenie and Summer Burke, whose support and loyalty ensured this project came to fruition.

Finally, thank you to you, the reader, the foodie, the discerning traveller – we hope you enjoy this book as much as we have enjoyed creating it.

Sarah Farag

FIJI IN BRIEF

With 333 islands and year-round warmth, Fiji's landscapes provide the perfect conditions for some incredible produce and locally-caught seafood. To the discerning traveller, Fiji is an untapped foodie paradise – a South Pacific haven where fresh, organic ingredients intermingle with cultural influences and cooking techniques to craft cuisine that is as healthy as it is exciting.

Fiji's cuisine reflects its rich multicultural history – blending spices, ingredients and cooking methods from Melanesian, Indian, Chinese and European cuisines. This unique fusion of influences along with its profusion of fresh seafood, exotic tropical fruit and seasonal vegetables makes for an exciting local food and drink scene.

Whether you're cruising the market for coconuts, enjoying smokey, succulent meat from the lovo pit, tucking into a fiery vegetable curry, sharing a bilo of kava, or savouring a coffee made from Fijian-grown beans, there is always something on the menu for everyone to enjoy.

The food scene in Fiji is growing, and at Fijian renowned luxury resorts sustainable food and beverage is a considered movement, with onsite farms at resorts, employment of local fishermen and the creation of dock-to-plate experiences for travellers. The culinary artisans elevate local bounty to create dishes that celebrate freshness and burst with the flavours of the islands.

www.fiji.com.fj

ABOUT KOKO & CHAI

Fijian-born sisters Komal and Sonali Swamy's shared passion for delicious food has fuelled their travels and inspired their unique flavour pairings, laying the foundations for Koko and Chai, their Auckland-based catering business

Koko and Chai delivers private chef experiences and events across New Zealand and the Pacific combining premium fresh ingredients and traditional Fijian flavours presented with a modern twist.

kokoandchai.com

GLOSSARY

baking powder a raising agent that is two parts cream of tartar to one part bicarbonate of soda.

butter we use salted butter unless stated otherwise. Unsalted or "sweet" butter has no salt added.

cassava an edible tuber from the cassava plant. This carbohydrate-dense vegetable is a major food crop across the Pacific world. It is used for savoury and sweet recipes. It must always be cooked first before eating.

chervil fragile, feathery chervil is one of the four herbs that make up the French fines herbes mixture (the others being parsley, chives and tarragon). Its subtle anise flavour creates an elegant note.

coconut
cream obtained commercially from the first pressing of the coconut flesh alone, without the addition of water.
desiccated concentrated, dried, unsweetened and finely shredded coconut flesh.
flaked dried flaked coconut flesh.
milk not the juice found inside the fruit, which is known as coconut water, but the diluted liquid from the second pressing of the white meat of the mature coconut.
oil extracted from the coconut flesh so you don't get any of the fibre, protein or carbohydrates present in the whole coconut. The best quality is virgin coconut oil, which is the oil pressed from the dried coconut flesh and doesn't include the use of solvents or other refining processes.

cornflour made from corn (100 per cent maize) or wheat: used as thickening agent.

couverture chocolate top-quality dark or milk chocolate with a high percentage of cocoa butter and cocoa liquor (known as cocoa solids), ranging from 50 to 90 per cent). The higher the cocoa content the more intense and bitter the chocolate flavour. Available from delicatessens and speciality food stores.

cream
crème fraiche a French variation of sour cream, it has a velvety texture and slightly tangy, nutty flavour. It can be boiled without curdling and is used in sweet and savoury dishes.
pouring also called pure or fresh cream. It has no additives and contains a minimum fat content of 35 per cent.
thickened a whipping cream with a thickener. It has a minimum fat content of 35 per cent.
cumquat a small oval or round citrus with little juice and a thin fragrant skin used to make preserves, pickles and infuse alcohol.

fenugreek seeds a mustard-coloured, hard, irregular formed seed that adds a nutty and a caramel-like flavour.

fillo pastry paper thin Greek pastry sold fresh or frozen (which has a tendency to crack). While working with it, ensure that the fillo is kept covered with a lightly damp tea towel to prevent it from drying out.

fish sauce also called nam pla or nuoc nam. Made from pulverised salted fermented fish, most often anchovies. Has a very pungent smell and strong taste, so use sparingly.

flour
plain unbleached wheat flour is the best for baking: the gluten content ensures a strong dough, which produces a light result.
self-raising all-purpose plain or wholemeal flour with baking powder and salt added. Also called self-rising flour.
tapioca derived from the starchy vegetable cassava root. Often used as an alternative to traditional wheat flours and starches.

galangal a rhizome resembling ginger in shape but with pink-hued skin. The flesh is denser and more fibrous than ginger, while the flavour is more delicate. Chop finely or thinly slice to use.

gelatine leaves leaf gelatine is tasteless and sets clearer than powdered gelatine, which is why it is preferred by chefs. It is graded according to setting strength, which is measured in "bloom". The higher the bloom strength the firmer the set. Each type has a different weight and set so it is advisable to use the type specified in the recipe.
gold-strength we use sheets that are 2.2gm each with a bloom strength of 200.
titanium-strength we use sheets that are 5gm each with a bloom strength of 120.

gelatine powder three teaspoons of dried gelatine (8g or one sachet) is about the same as four gelatine leaves. The two types are interchangeable, but leaf gelatine gives a much clearer mixture than dried gelatine.

ginger, fresh also called green or root ginger; the thick gnarled root of a tropical plant. Can be kept, peeled, covered with dry sherry in a jar and refrigerated, or frozen in an airtight container.

glutinous rice a type of rice grown mainly in Southeast and East Asia and the eastern parts of South Asia. The grains are opaque with a very low amylose content and are sticky, or glue-like, when cooked. Used in many forms of Asian cooking, from savoury dishes to desserts.

Grana Padano Italy's most produced cheese. A full-bodied hard cheese with a grainy, crystalline texture. Aged for a minimum of nine months, Grana Padano matures more quickly than Parmigiano-Reggiano. It matures in three stages: 9-16 months when it is more delicate in flavour, softer in texture and has a pale yellow colour; 16-20 months when it is grainier with notes of butter, hay and dried fruit; and over 20 months when it has a rich buttery flavour and crystals are present.

grapeseed oil an oil with a high-burn point, favoured by chefs due its neutral taste.

hearts of palm canned palm hearts in brine, available from South American grocers and continental delis.

kombu a form of edible kelp widely used in Japanese cooking to make broths. It can also be pickled, eaten fresh and deep-fried.

lemon balm a soft-leaf herb from the mint family wtih a subtle lemon scent.

lemongrass a tall, clumping, lemon-smelling and -tasting, sharp-edged aromatic tropical grass. The white lower part of the stem is used in many Southeast Asian dishes.

makrut lime leaf sold fresh, dried or frozen, it looks like two glossy dark green leaves joined end to end, forming a rounded hourglass shape. A strip of fresh lime peel may be substituted for each makrut lime leaf.

mirin a Japanese straw-coloured cooking wine made of glutinous rice and alcohol.

miso fermented soybean paste. There are many types, each with its own aroma, flavour, colour and texture. It can be refrigerated in an airtight container for up to a year. Generally, the darker the miso, the saltier the taste and denser the texture.

'nduja a soft, spreadable fermented pork salume, spiked with fiery Calabrian chillies.

nori sheets a type of dried seaweed used in Japanese cooking as a flavouring, garnish or for sushi. Sold in thin sheets, plain or toasted (yaki-nori).

potato starch derived from crushed dried potatoes to form a fine white flour. It is used as a thickener and to create crisp batters and is gluten free.

radicchio a red-leafed Italian chicory with a refreshing bitter taste that's eaten raw or grilled. Comes in varieties named after their places of origin, such as round-headed Verona or long-headed Treviso.

rock lobsters buy whole lobsters alive. Never accept a dead, raw lobster as the flesh spoils rapidly after death. They should be heavy for their size and smell fresh.

Sichuan peppercorns also called Szechuan or Chinese pepper, native to the Sichuan province of China. A mildly hot spice that comes from the prickly ash tree. Although not related to the peppercorn family, the small, red-brown aromatic Sichuan berries look like black peppercorns and have a distinctive peppery-lemon flavour and aroma.

shallots
golden also called French shallots or eschalots. Small and elongated with

a brown skin.
red shallots red skinned, they are drier and more strongly flavoured than European shallots.

Shaoxing also called shao hsing or Chinese rice wine. It is made from fermented rice, wheat, sugar and salt with a 13.5 per cent alcohol content. Inexpensive and found in Asian food shops. If unavailable, replace with mirin or sherry.

shiso the Japanese name for a popular Southeast Asian herb. A member of the mint family, it has jagged leaves and a flavour similar to basil and coriander, with subtle hints of cumin and cloves. Served fresh or pickled, and commonly used to garnish sushi and other Japanese dishes.

sugar
coconut made from the nectar of coconut blossoms from coconut palms, with a caramel taste and crumb-like texture.
golden caster sugar a fine granulated sugar made from unrefined sugar cane or beets. Light golden in colour and similar in texture to regular white caster sugar, it has a subtle buttery, caramel flavour. If a recipe calls for regular white caster sugar, you can substitute for golden caster sugar.
palm also called nam tan pip, jaggery, jawa or gula melaka. Made from the sap of the sugar palm tree. Light brown to black in colour and usually sold in rock-hard cakes. Substitute brown sugar if unavailable.

tamarind paste the tamarind tree produces clusters of hairy brown pods, each of which is filled with seeds and a viscous pulp that are dried and pressed into the blocks of tamarind found in Asian food shops. Gives a sweet-sour, slightly astringent taste to marinades, pastes, sauces and dressings.

tamarind purée (or paste) the commercial result of the distillation of tamarind juice into a condensed, compacted purée.

Thai basil also known as bai horapha, this is different from holy basil and sweet basil in look and taste. With smaller leaves and purplish stems, it has a slight aniseed taste and is a typical flavour in Thai cuisine.

vinegar
chardonnay made from chardonnay wine. Fruity with a delicate, complex flavour.
rice vinegar Chinese and Japanese vinegars are less acidic than Western ones, and Thai vinegar is milder still. They are made from rice wine or sake and have a subtle tang with a hint of sweetness.
sherry a Spanish vinegar made from fermenting sherry wine. It has a deep, complex flavour and subtle caramel notes, with less acidity than red or white wine vinegar.

white chocolate strictly speaking, not chocolate as it contains no cocoa solid. It is a mixture of cocoa butter, milk solids, sugar and flavourings. The best white chocolate for cooking is couverture white chocolate, which contains high proportions of the aforementioned ingredients.

witlof also called Belgian endive or chicory. It has green or red leaves with tightly packed, cigar-shaped heads, and is crunchy with a mildly bitter flavour.

xanthan gum derived from fermenting sugar with a form of bacteria. Used as a multi-use stabiliser and thickener. It has no discernible taste and a pleasing mouthfeel.

yeast (dried and fresh) a raising agent used in dough-making. Granular yeast (7gm sachets) and fresh compressed yeast (20gm blocks) can almost always be substituted one for the other.

yellowtail kingfish a meaty-textured fish with a medium level of oiliness. It is available wild and farmed, and frequently sold by the Japanese name of Hiramasa.

yuzu originating in East Asia, yuzu is believed to be a hybrid of sour mandarin and a slow-growing tropical lemon. The fruit has uneven skin and a tart flavour that recalls grapefruit but with mandarin overtones, and a highly aromatic perfume. Rarely eaten as a fruit, yuzu's aromatic zest and juice are often used as seasoning. It is an integral ingredient in the Japanese sauce ponzu.

COOK'S NOTES

Measures & equipment

- All cup and spoon measures are level and based on Australian metric measures.
- Eggs have an average weight of 59gm unless otherwise specified.
- Fruit and vegetables are washed, peeled and medium-sized unless specified.
- Oven temperatures are for conventional ovens and need to be adjusted for fan-forced ovens.
- Pans are medium-sized and heavy-based; cake tins are stainless steel, unless otherwise specified.

Cooking tips

- When seasoning food, we use sea salt and freshly ground pepper.
- To blanch an ingredient, cook it briefly in boiling water, then drain. To refresh, plunge in iced water, then drain.
- We recommend using free-range eggs, chicken and pork. We use female pork for preference.
- Makrut lime leaves are also known as kaffir lime leaves.
- Unless specified, neutral oil means any of grapeseed, canola, sunflower or vegetable oil.
- To dry-roast spices, cook them in a dry pan, stirring over medium-high heat until fragrant. Cooking time varies.
- Non-reactive bowls are made from glass, ceramic or plastic. Use them in preference to metal bowls when marinating to prevent the acid in marinades reacting with metal and imparting a metallic taste.
- RSPCA Australia's advice for killing crustaceans humanely is to render them insensible by placing them in the freezer (under 4°C) until the tail or outer mouth parts can be moved without resistance; crustaceans must then be killed quickly by cutting through the centreline of the head and thorax. For crabs, insert a knife into the head. This process destroys the nerve centres of the animal.
- All herbs are fresh, with leaves and tender stems used, unless specified.
- Eggwash is lightly beaten egg used for glazing or sealing.
- Sugar syrup is made of equal parts sugar and water, unless otherwise specified. Bring mixture to the boil to dissolve sugar, remove from heat and cool before use.
- Acidulated water is a mixture of water and lemon juice.
- To sterilise jars and lids, run them through the hot rinse cycle in a dishwasher, or wash them in hot soapy water, rinse well, place on a tray in a cold oven and heat at 120°C for 30 minutes.
- To blind bake, line a pastry-lined tart tin with baking paper, then fill it with weights (ceramic weights, rice and dried beans work best).
- To clarify butter, cook it over low heat until the fat and the milk solids separate. Strain off the clear butter and discard the milk solids. You will lose about 20 per cent of the volume in milk solids.

INDEX

A
ARTICHOKES
Artichoke purée 63

B
BEEF
Beef tartare with capers, mustard, cornichon and egg yolks............................78
Eye fillet with mushroom, artichoke, blueberry and burnt butter emulsion 63
BLUEBERRIES
Macerated blueberries.......63

C
CASSAVA
Cassava cake......................120
CEVICHE
Ceviche of Spanish mackerel and passionfruit.............105
Kokoda ceviche...................116
Prawn ceviche (ura konda taki)......................................46
CHICKEN
Chicken sang choi bau 32
Steamed prawn and chicken dumplings with black vinegar sauce...................74
Thai green chicken curry with basil palm heart................18
CHOCOLATE
Kini's chocolate croissants 148
Milk chocolate miso semifreddo with coffee crémeux............................ 92
Rich chocolate terrine with chocolate sponge and rum topping 191
White chocolate passionfruit mousse with coconut caramel sauce................162

CITRUS
Citrus hibiscus granita and coconut ice-cream........ 176
Citrus salad........................... 50
Tarte au citron.....................106
CLAMS
Kaikoso clams in lime and soy dressing 147
CRAB
Chilli mud crab.....................35
CUCUMBERS
Cucumber salad................158
Smashed cucumbers..........49
CUMQUAT
Cumquat jam..........................21
CURRIES
Fijian fish curry...................132
Thai green chicken curry with basil palm heart................18

F
FISH
Blackened snapper with cucumber salad.............158
Ceviche of Spanish mackerel and passionfruit.............105
Fijian fish curry...................132
Fish and prawn island sliders 172
Goldband snapper, kai mussels and calamari with lolo sauce and crustacean oil.................. 131
Grilled fish Wakaya with spinach salad, thyme sauce and red wine sauce 119
Kingfish sashimi with almond cream, lemongrass, makrut-lime leaf oil 64
Seared tuna with Fijian-style potato curry 187

Smoked Spanish mackerel with macadamia milk, salted radish and dill oil 91
Spiced rum tuna gravlax... 50
Steamed snapper with ginger, soy and sesame.............................. 77

G
GAZPACHO
Yasawa gazpacho..............188

H
HALWA
Halwa crème brûlée with cardamom ice-cream... 135

I
ICE-CREAM
Citrus hibiscus granita and coconut ice-cream........ 176

K
KIWIFRUIT
Fermented kiwifruit 60
Marinated kiwifruit.............. 60

L
LOBSTER
Barbecued lobster with 'nduja butter and toasted nori 36
Grilled lobster with Fijian asparagus and light coconut curry sauce.....102
Island lobster salad with ginger-lime aïoli and vudi crisps................................ 144

Lobster salad with steamed potatoes and lemon vinaigrette 175

P
PAPAYA
Green papaya pad Thai.....22
PORK
Pork belly with cumquat jam, apple and walnuts 21
PRAWN
Drunken prawns...................49
Fish and prawn island sliders 172
Lemongrass prawn skewers with Thai green curry cappuccino 161
Prawn ceviche (ura konda taki)......................................46
Steamed prawn and chicken dumplings with black vinegar sauce...................74

S
SALADS
Citrus salad........................... 50
SCALLOPS
Cured scallops with fermented marinated kiwifruit.............................. 60
SEAWEED
Seaweed tartlet with black truffle, mushrooms, warm potato and sweet peas 88

Published in 2024 by Are Media Books, Australia. Are Media Books is a division of Are Media Pty Ltd.

Editor Joanna Hunkin

Food Director Sophia Young

Creative Director Jacqui Triggs

Contributing designers
Hannah Blackmore, Nigel Cruickshank

Managing Editor Anna McCooe

Contributing Editor Stephanie Kistner

Content Editors Chantal Gibbs,
Michelle Oalin (recipes)

Books Director David Scotto

A catalogue record for this
book is available from the
National Library of Australia.
ISBN 978-1-76122-186-6

FOOD PHOTOGRAPHY

Photographer John Paul Urizar

Stylist Olivia Blackmore, Lucy Busuttil

Food preparation Rebecca Lyall

Drinks Matches Samantha Payne

TRAVEL PHOTOGRAPHY

Oliver Bolch, Jason Busch, Jay Clue.
Maria Cruces, Holger Leue, Klaus
Lorke, Maria Louw, Hamilton Lund, Brett
Monroe Garner, Chris Park, Markus
Ravic, Rob Rickman, Tom Vierus, Chris
Williams/Blackbox

Published by Are Media Books,
a division of Are Media Pty Limited,
54 Park St, Sydney; GPO Box 4088,
Sydney, NSW 2001, Australia
Phone +61 2 9282 8000
aremediabooks.com.au

Published in partnership with
Southern Crossings
southern-crossings.com

To order books
Phone 1300 322 007 (within Australia)
Or online at *aremediabooks.com.au*

Printed in China by
CC Offset Printing Co., Ltd

SOUTHERN CROSSINGS